Prayer and Revival

PRAYER AND REVIVAL

E. M. BOUNDS

Edited by Darrel D. King

BAKER BOOK HOUSE
Grand Rapids, Michigan 49516

Copyright © 1993 by Baker Books
a division of Baker Book House Company
P.O. Box 6287, Grand Rapids, MI 49516-6287

ISBN: 0-8010-1035-7

Second printing, March 1994

Printed in the United States of America

Contents

Preface

IT is from the writings of the assistant editor of the *Christian Advocate* of the general organ of the Methodist Episcopal Church, South, that this volume is comprised. These are jewels that have been locked away in a treasure chest. Each one shines with holy life for every person who will read, receive, prayerfully consider, and embrace it.

This volume is addressed to pastors. Though it will be enlightening and edifying for the whole church, I have assembled the articles that would be primarily of interest to pastors. It is appropriate that these jewels would be in the treasure chest of E. M. Bounds for his beloved fellow pastors throughout the ages. His was a heart of compassion for fellow pastors. He wept for the cities of the nation, he travailed for the churches in America and around the world, his heart was touched by evangelical churches coast to coast and around the world. Dr. Bounds shares with men of God from the heart of a man of God. Open this treasure chest and examine the jewels therein.

I wish to express sincere gratitude, appreciation, and love for co-laborers that helped me so diligently in this project: Kathy Summers, typist; Jenny Powell, free-lance writer and editor, Atlanta, Georgia; and Hazel Luna, librarian, United Methodist, Nashville, Tennessee. I would also like to express my appreciation for their encouragement to Rev. Chester Estes Jr., director of Prayertime Ministries, Union, Mississippi; Rev. James Hamlett, pastor of West Side General Baptist Church,

St. Louis, Missouri; Dr. Ben Rogers, professor at Luther Rice Seminary; and Mike Gibson of Atlanta, Georgia.

A very special thanks to Jan, my wife, and to Beth and Sara, our daughters, for their sacrifice of my time with them.

Yours for revival in this generation.

Darrel D. King, director
E. M. Bounds School
of Prayer and Revivalism

A Biography of E. M. Bounds

Then He said to me, "Son of man, stand on your feet that I may speak with you!" And as He spoke to me the Spirit entered me and set me on my feet; and I heard Him speaking to me. Then He said to me, "Son of man, I am sending you to the sons of Israel, to a rebellious people who have rebelled against Me; they and their fathers have transgressed against Me to this very day. And I am sending you to them who are stubborn and obstinate children; and you shall say to them, 'Thus says the Lord God.' As for them, whether they listen or not—for they are a rebellious house—they will know that a prophet has been among them. And you, son of man, neither fear them nor fear their words, though thistles and thorns are with you and you sit on scorpions; neither fear their words nor be dismayed at their presence, for they are a rebellious house. But you shall speak My words to them whether they listen or not, for they are rebellious."

[Ezek. 2:1–7 NASB]

THE prophet of prayer was born to Thomas Jefferson (T. J.) and Harriet Saphronia Bounds. In a small log cabin beside the banks of the Salt River in Marion County, Missouri, the crying voice of Edward McKendree Bounds was first heard on August 15, 1835.

During his first year, the family of E. M. Bounds moved and helped establish the new county of Shelby. The Bounds family's influence became evident right from the start. T. J. Bounds surveyed Shelbyville, the county seat, and he became a leading figure in the social, economic, and religious fiber of the town, which was nestled in the rolling hills of northeastern Missouri.

E. M. Bounds had a secure childhood in the little town of Shelbyville. When E. M. was 15 years old, his father died and left his family financially stable and living in a prosperous community.

With his older brother, Charles, E. M. decided to go to California to profit from the great gold rush of 1849. After spending a year in the El Dorado canyon area, the Bounds brothers traveled north and finally returned to Missouri. They returned without success in the gold rush, but the experience strengthened their Christian character.

Before long, E. M. Bounds began studying law. During this time, a great spiritual awakening swept across the United States. In that time of spiritual bliss, E. M. Bounds felt the call to ministry. Abandoning his law practice and embracing the heavenly call, he attended seminary in Palmyra, Missouri. His ministry began in 1859 when he presented himself to the Methodist Episcopal Church, South, Conference in Missouri. On trial, he was assigned the Monticello circuit north of Hannibal. The following year he was assigned to an influential church in Brunswick, Missouri. This church was being pastored at the time by the famous W. G. Caples. As this great man was being assigned to another location, he brought E. M. Bounds to pastor his church. Bounds came to his new pastorate, just as the northern region of Missouri was being ravaged by the escalating Civil War. With the occupation of the Union forces, the fighting of the Confederate forces, and the plundering of the renegades, the populace of this region was being raped, plundered, and abused. In the midst of this chaos, Bounds was arrested and accused of being a Confederate sympathizer. Because he would not swear allegiance to the Union or post bond, Bounds was incarcerated and moved to St. Louis to serve time during the harsh Missouri winter. He spent the Christmas of 1862 incarcerated and abused, but after two weeks in the Gratiot Street prison, he was officially exiled from Missouri by General Curtis, never to return as long as there was conflict.

Eventually he was moved by Union forces to Memphis, Tennessee. He was sent to Washington, Arkansas, where he was released. He then traveled to Jacksonville, Mississippi, and walked more than one hundred miles to Camp Pritchard where he was sworn in as a Confederate chaplain, joining forces with Dr. Sterling Price, a Christian friend and neighbor from Brunswick. On May 13, 1863, he was assigned the chaplaincy of the Missouri Third Infantry. He served in this capacity, not only with the Missouri Third but with other divisions. Reports spread of his effectiveness in bringing spiritual influence to the camps. While traveling with the forces, as the troops would bivouac, he would find a place to preach, often in neighboring churches. At each place, God would move mightily in revival and conversions. This continued even into the trenches at the siege of Vicksburg, Mississippi, and Atlanta, Georgia. Here the intensity of revival was such that it influenced General John B. Hood. He and nine of his officers were confirmed in St. Luke's Episcopal Church. Bishop Henry Law presided over the service and the pastor, Dr. Charles Quintard, assisted.

After the fall of Atlanta, General Hood made a desperate thrust toward Nashville. Great tragedy struck the troops in Franklin, Tennessee. The blood of gallant men mingled on the battlefield where the Missouri forces were so ravaged that they could no longer fight as a strong force. When the battle in Franklin ended, Bounds, though wounded, remained with the casualties to try to help them in their agony and pain. The forces moved on to Nashville in a failed attempt to take it from Union forces, and when the Confederate troops moved back through Franklin in retreat, Bounds came to a decision to stay with the casualties, even though this decision would inevitably lead to his capture and incarceration.

After a six-month incarceration in Nashville, Bounds could not get Franklin off his mind and heart. He returned to the ravaged town where the populace had been decimated by the war. They had given the last of their food, clothing, and hospitality to the soldiers in that tragic battle. Bounds returned to a little church whose members had been scattered. He began to pray and sing praises to God and, as a hen with her chicks, drew the people back together. Before long, they began to grow into a vibrant church.

After a successful pastorate in Franklin, Bounds was called to serve in Selma, Alabama. In a community where he had preached as a chaplain, he now came as the pastor. Here again God poured out his blessings, not only on the Word of God but also on the man of God. Church Street Methodist Episcopal Church, South, where Bounds was pastor, took on a vibrancy tinged with great expectancy. After three years, he was moved from Selma to Eufaula, Alabama, to commence a work in another struggling church. A relocation of the church was required and Bounds led that great church to build a building with a steeple so high that it became the testimony of God's faithfulness to southeast Alabama and the southwest region of Georgia.

He met his first wife, Emmie E. Barnett, while pastoring the Methodist Episcopal Church, South. After four years, he was asked by Bishop Marvin in the St. Louis Conference to pastor the St. Peter's Methodist Episcopal Church, South, in the rapidly growing city of St. Louis, Missouri. He returned to his beloved home state to pastor this church. After four years, Bishop Marvin asked him to pastor the First Methodist Episcopal Church, South, which he did for one year. He came with a high pietistic standard, a clear declaration of God's Word, an example to be emulated, and a power that moved the church to return to the moorings that had built that great testimony in the heart of St. Louis. Bounds then returned to St. Peter's Methodist Episcopal Church, South, and continued his ministry. During this pastorate, after ten years of marriage, God took home his beloved Emmie and left him with two daughters and one son. Harriet Barnett, Emmie's cousin, later became Bounds's wife and his helpmate throughout his remaining years.

While pastoring in St. Louis, he was asked to serve as associate editor of the *St. Louis Christian Advocate* of the Methodist Episcopal Church, South, in Missouri. In this position he became a leader in calling the people of God back to God, not only among the Methodists but among others who read his editorials. He also traveled throughout the region, speaking and preaching in conferences and meetings, impacting churches and communities.

As his reputation for his pietistic stand spread, it was noted in the Methodist Episcopal Church, South, Conference. On May 22, 1890, Bounds was elected to become associate editor of the *Christian Advocate* in Nashville. This national paper for the Methodist Episcopal Church, South, had an impact on all churches that subscribed to it. He served effectively, boldly, and strongly his beloved Methodist Episcopal Church, South, authoring numerous articles that impacted churches of that day. As a prophet, Bounds had followers and detractors. There were those who had ears to hear, who listened and complied, and those who did not hear and became alienated and resentful toward Bounds.

A great revivalist once said that you either receive and respond to a prophet or you destroy him. So it was with Bounds. As he stood with a strong pietistic conviction of righteousness, opposition began to grow. The opposition did not come fully against Bounds but was evident among Christians in political, worldly, and merchandising attitudes that he could not and would not condone. During the national Methodist Episcopal Church, South, conference in Memphis in 1894, Bounds left because of his convictions. Upon returning to Nashville, he concluded his responsibilities there and then moved to his wife's home in Washington, Georgia.

In this beautiful antebellum community, Bounds continued an itinerant revival ministry. It was not Methodist leaders who came to Washington but men of humble hearts, desiring to know God in a righteous piety who came to this great man of God and sat at his feet. Many pastors called him to minister to their flocks, and his ministry of writing continued. At the conclusion of many hours in prayer, he would jot down a few notes on paper. Finally he produced a first volume called *Preacher and Prayer.* Other volumes followed.

On August 24, 1913, the voice that rang so loud in the valleys of Missouri was silenced on earth in the mountains of Georgia, to be activated in glory to praise Holy God, to magnify the Lord Jesus Christ, and to embrace the Holy Spirit. Even after his death, a dear friend, Dr. H. W. Hodge, worked diligently with the little pieces of paper, paragraphs, and articles and continued to assemble volumes that have become a library on prayer and spiritual matters.

1

Watch and Pray
June 17, 1890

OUR Savior exhorted his disciples on at least two occasions to watch and pray. (See Mark 13:33 and 14:38.) Hence, we know that these two duties belong together. We must watch while we pray and pray while we watch. Paul repeats this exhortation in two of his letters. He writes to the Colossians: "Continue in prayer and watch in the same with thanksgiving." And to the Ephesians: "Praying always with all prayer and supplication in the Spirit and watching thereunto."

A great deal of the praying in our day is formal and unprofitable. We separate these two things that the Lord united. This is as if we should try to have air without oxygen, or water without hydrogen. Watching is needful before we pray, while we pray, and after we pray. It is the preparation for the accompaniment and of the application of all true prayer. Let us look at it in this three-fold relation.

We must watch for opportunities for prayer. Some people pray only at set times, as a matter of habit. They repeat the Lord's Prayer and similar stereotyped supplications morning and evening and think that is praying. But it is only saying prayers. It is using vain repetitions as the heathen do. Paul tells us to be "praying always," and one of our hymns declares that

"prayer is the Christian's vital breath." Now, if breathing were
voluntary—if we had to think about it in order to do it—would
we not be watching for chances to breathe while talking or
walking? Just so, since praying does not take care of itself like
breathing, we must watch all the day for quiet moments when
the heart can go out to God in supplication. If we finish a task
we should pause long enough to thank God for his help and
to ask him to go with us as we turn to the next day. O how
much richer our lives would be in Christian experience and
in Christian hope if we were continually watching unto prayer!
Again, we must watch for objects to pray for. Prayer, to amount
to anything, must be definite and specific. To kneel down at
night and ask God to comfort all who mourn is so vague and
general that we must say the words without any deep feeling.
But if we have sought out some sufferer and tried to comfort
him, we will pray for him a real prayer—one that will go from
our heart to the heart of God. In regard to the impenitent
around us, if we sought to interest some soul in the great salvation during the day, how earnestly will we commend that
soul to God in our closet of prayer at home? And more than
all, we must be watching our own hearts, noting the temptations that assail us and the sins that most easily beset us, that
we may know what to pray for.

In prayer we seek for God's blessing on ourselves and others.
We might say that it is not necessary to specify for God knows
all things. When I cry, "Lead me not into temptation," he
understands better than I do what my special temptations are.
When I ask him to have mercy on sinners, he knows whom I
mean without my naming them. But it would be just as reasonable to say, since God knows all things why pray to him at
all? Prayer is the appointed channel of his grace. He will be
inquired of. He says, "Ask, and ye shall receive," and the asking
cannot be real, earnest, and hearty unless it is specific.

In each of our large cities there is a fire department. In
engine houses there are men, horses, hose-carriages, and
engines ready to go at a moment's warning. But they do not

go hunting for fires. They wait until they are summoned. On a tower in the center of the city stands a watchman. He is looking north and south, east and west. As soon as he sees the smoke of a conflagration he sounds the alarm, and at once the fire department is in motion. The watchman tells them by his signal just where to go, and so no time is lost. Now everybody can see how necessary the watching is in this case. Somewhat like it is the necessity for watching in regard to prayer. True, God is not dependent on the signal of the watchman in order to know where his grace is needed, but he has chosen to give it only in response to the prayer of faith, and such prayer must be definite and specific.

We must watch while we pray for it is then that Satan will marshal his subtlest temptations. He will use the law of association and try to fill our minds with wandering thoughts. He will persuade us, if he can, that there is merit in our prayers and that God ought to answer them because they are so earnest and fitly phrased. Yes, we must watch against carnal desires—asking for things that we may consume upon our lusts. As a general during a battle watches every movement of the foe, as he is alert to detect any new strategy, so we must be in our prayers.

Finally, we must watch for answers to our prayers. If a man goes to a friend to ask a favor of him, he does not say, "Mr. A., will you lend me a hundred dollars?" and then hurry away before Mr. A. has a chance to reply. No indeed. He watches the face of him to whom he applies, that he may read the answer before it is spoken. And then he will listen for the uttered response. And if that response is vague or hesitating, he will repeat and press his request. Not to wait upon one from whom we expect a favorable answer shows that we are not really earnest and hopeful. If a man who went to Washington seeking an office from the president should hand in his application and then go away without waiting to see how it was received, his prospects for success would be very small indeed.

Now, we cannot watch God's face as we do that of a human friend, but there is a way in which we can show that we are waiting on him with expectation. For instance, suppose that a Christian prays earnestly and in faith for the outpouring of the Spirit upon the heart of an impenitent friend. If he expects that God will hear and answer, will he not go to that friend next day and talk with him to see if his heart is newly interested in spiritual things? The archer who shoots an arrow at a mark watches to see if he has hit it. He does not shoot for the sake of shooting but to accomplish a definite result, and he shows his interest in that result. So should we. The failure to do this reveals the formalism of our prayers. When we ask for something, we do not really expect to get it. If we did, we would be ever watching as we pray that we might see the answer in God's providence, or feel its throbbings in our hearts.

2

Desire in Prayer
October 4, 1890

FAITH is the source, life, and projecting force of prayer. Prayer is dependent on the name, merits, and intercession of Christ. Passing by these fundamentals, conditions, and vital forces in prayer, we come to the basis of prayer, which is seated in the human heart. It is not simply our need, for if that were prayer we would be ever praying, for we are always needy. The basis of prayer is not a wish, a passing impulse, a hasty glance heavenward. Desire is the basis of prayer: "Whatsoever things ye *desire* when ye pray," said Christ.

Desire is said to be the will in action. It is a strong sensation excited in the mind by some good. Desire exalts the object and fixes the mind on it. Desire has choice and fixedness and flame in it. Prayer based on desire is explicit and specific. The one praying knows his need and feels and sees the thing demanded.

Prayer is not a performance; it is not an indefinite, widespread clamor. It is spurred by desire that kindles the soul and holds its attention on the object desired. Prayer ought to be part of our spiritual habits, but it ceases to be prayer when it is carried on by habit only. It is the depth and intensity of the spiritual desires that give depth and intensity to prayer. Desire gives fervor to prayer. The soul cannot be listless when some great desire fixes and inflames it. Desire gives importunity, an urgency that will not be denied but stays and pleads and will not go till its desires are met. Strong desires make strong prayers. Desire is much helped by contemplation. Meditation on our condition, our needs, and God's readiness and ability makes desire grow.

The secret of unanswered barren prayers is found in the weakness of our desires. The neglect of prayer is the fearful token of dead spiritual desires. The soul has turned away from God when desire after him no longer presses it to the prayer closet. Though one may pray without desire, there can be no true praying if desire is absent. We catalogue many things in our prayers—we cover a large area of ground—but do our desires make up the catalogue? Do our desires map out the region covered by our prayers? Desire is intense and narrow. It cannot spread itself over a wide field. It wants a few things and it wants them badly, so badly that nothing but God's will can content it with anything else.

"Blessed are they which do hunger and thirst after righteousness: for they shall be filled." This desire that has entered into the spiritual appetite and clamors to be satisfied is the basis of a prayer that fills us by its answer.

Do not our prayers often lie in the sickly regions of a mere wish or the feeble expression of a memorized concern or want? Sometimes our prayers are but stereotyped editions of set phrases and decent proportions whose freshness and life went out years ago.

It is the flame of a present and filling desire that mounts to God. It is the ardor created by desire that burns its way to the throne of mercy and gains its plea. It is the pertinacity of desire that gives triumph to the conflict in a great struggle of prayer. It is the burden of a weighty desire that sobers and makes restless and reduces to quiet the soul in its mighty wrestlings. It is desire that arms prayer with a thousand pleas and robes it with invincible courage and all-conquering force.

The Syrophoenician woman exemplifies desire that is consistent and invulnerable in its intensity and boldness. The importunate widow is desire gaining its end despite obstacles that would be insurmountable by feebler impulses.

We fail more in desire than in the outward performances of prayer. We keep the form, but the inner life fades and dies. Are not the feebleness of our desires for God, for the Holy Ghost, and for all the fullness of Christ the cause of our little and languished praying? Do we feel the inward pantings of desire after these heavenly treasures? Do our inbred groanings of desire stir our souls to mighty wrestlings? The flame burns low. The boiling heat has been tempered to a respectable lukewarmness. Have we the desire that presses us to communion with God filled with unutterable burnings and that holds us there through the hours of an intense and soul-stirred supplication? Our hearts need to be worked on, not only to get the evil out, but to get the good in; and the foundation and inspiration to the incoming good is desire. This holy and fervid flame in the soul awakens heaven's attention, and all heaven's inexhaustible stores are waiting to supply these heaven-born desires.

Revivals That Stay
December 6, 1890

REVIVALS are among the charter rights of the church. They are the evidences of its divinity, the tokens of God's presence, the witness of his power. The frequency and power of these extraordinary seasons of grace are the tests and preservers of the vital force in the church. The church that is not visited by these seasons is as sterile in all spiritual products as a desert and cannot meet the designs of God's church. Such churches may have all the show and parade of life, but it is only a painted life.

The preacher whose experience is not marked by these inflows of great grace may question with anxious scrutiny whether he is in grace. The preacher whose ministry does not over and over again find its climax of success and power in these gracious visitations of God may well doubt the genuineness of his call, or be disquieted as to its continuance.

The Methodist Church is the child of a revival, and its marvelous career finds the source of its unparalleled results in its revival element.

Revival brings life to the individual as well as to the church. Revivals are not simply the reclamation of a backslidden church. They do secure this result, but their highest end is not this. Revivals invigorate and mature by one mighty act the feeble saints; they also cause the advanced ones of God's elect to pass on to sublimer regions of faith and experience. They are the fresh baptisms—the more powerful consecration of a waiting, willing, working church to a profounder willingness and a mightier ability for a mightier work. These revivals are the pitched battles and the decisive victories for God, when the slain of the Lord are many and his triumph glorious.

There are counterfeit revivals well executed and well calculated to deceive the most wary. These are deceptive and superficial with many unpleasant, entertaining, delusive features that distinguish them from the genuine ones. The pain of penitence, the shame of guilt, the sorrow and humiliation from sin, the fear of hell—these marks of the genuine are lacking in the counterfeit. The test of a genuine revival is found in its staying qualities. The counterfeit is but a winter spurt, as evanescent and fitful as the morning cloud or early dew—both soon gone—and the sun but the hotter for the mockery of the cloud and the fleeting dew. These surface revivals do more harm than good, like a surface thaw in midwinter, which only increases the hardness and roughness of tomorrow's freeze. The genuine revival goes to the bottom of things; the sword is not swaddled in cotton or festooned with flowers but pierces to the dividing asunder of soul and spirit and of joints and marrow.

A genuine revival marks an era in the life of the church. It plants the germs of the great spiritual principles that grow and mature through all the changing seasons that follow. Revival seasons are favoring seasons, when the tides of salvation are at their flood, when all the waves and winds move heavenward: jubilee days of emancipation and return and rapture. The church needs revivals. It cannot live, it cannot do its work, without revivals that will lift it above the sands of worldliness that shallow the current and impede the sailing. These revivals give new life to the great spiritual principles, which are worn threadbare in many a church. It is true that in the most thorough work some will fall away, but when the work is genuine and far reaching, as it ought to be, the waste will scarcely be felt in the presence of the good that remains.

The effects of a revival will stay if that revival springs from within the church—the natural outgrowth of the spiritual condition of the church. So-called revivals that do not spring from the repentance, faith, and prayers of the church may be induced by foreign and outside forces. Many of the religious movements of the day have no foundation in the travailing throes of the church. By outside pressure, the presence and reputation of an evangelist and imported singers and imported songs, an interest is awakened, a passing impression made, but these are quite different from the concern aroused by the presence of God and the mighty power of his almighty Spirit. In the manufactured revival there is an interest that does not deepen into conviction, that is not subdued into awe, that cannot be molded into prayer nor agitated by fears. There is the utter absence of the spirit of prayer, the spirit of repentance has no place, lightness and frivolity reign, tears are strange and unwelcome visitors. The church members, instead of being on their knees in intercession or mingling their wrestling cries with the wrestling penitents or joining in rapturous praise with their rapturous deliverance, are simply spectators of a pleasing entertainment in which they have but a momentary interest. From a spiritual standpoint, the results of such a revival are far below zero. A revival needs a burdened church, a burdened pastor, and burdened penitents.

The results of revival will be gracious and abiding when they spring from the spiritual contact of pastor and church with God. A season of fasting and prayer and of deep humiliation and confession are the conditions from which a genuine and powerful work springs.

The nature of the preaching is of the first importance. Its character will guide the converts and determine the depth of the work. The word of God in its purity and strength must be given. The law of God in its spiritual demands must arouse the conscience and pierce and lay bare the heart. If there ever is a time for sentimental anecdotes, for the exercise of wit; if

the preacher is ever justified in pausing to soften the sympa-
thies or inflame the fancy, it is not at this period.

The object must not be superficial—working on tender emo-
tions—but it must be to convict the conscience, search out the
sinner and expose his sins, alarm the guilty soul, and intensify
the faith and effort of the believer. The Word of God is the
imperishable and vitalizing seed. The Spirit of God is the breath
of spring, and it must blow, but it must have seed on which to
breathe and create life. The Word of God is the quickening
energy that is to be let loose. The Word of God is the sword of
the Spirit. The sword must be unsheathed and it must cut with
both edges.

The spirit of prayer must be the one evident and prevailing
spirit. The spirit of prayer is but the spirit of faith, the spirit
of reverence, the spirit of supplication. This must be main-
tained and increased. This spirit holds in its keeping the success
of the word and the power of the Holy Ghost; as the spirit of
prayer fails, these fail. If the spirit of prayer is absent or is
quenched, God is not in the assembly. He comes and stays only
in the cloud of glory formed by the incense of a church whose
flame of prayer is ascending to him. All genuine revivals are
simply God coming with great grace to his church. The revival
that springs from heart contact of the church with God, that
is directed and intensified by the pure preaching of the pure
Word of God, and in which, and through which, prayer, mighty
prayer, prevails is a revival that will stay.

4

Rejected Prayers
December 20, 1890

ALL prayers may be divided into three classes: answered, unanswered, and rejected. The Bible and Christian experience are filled with instances of the first class. Abraham, Jacob, Joseph, Moses, Samuel, David, and many others, men and women, received responses to their petitions. In the New Testament, Zacharias and Elizabeth, Simeon and Anna, Paul and Silas, Peter and Cornelius prayed and were answered. And we read of another

> who in the days of his flesh, when he had offered up prayers and supplications with strong crying and tears unto him that was able to save him from death, and was heard in that he feared.
>
> [Hebrews 5:7]

These examples serve to illustrate the fact that prayers are not in vain. Often the answers come in time to be known by those who prayed. Sometimes the answer is sent before the prayer has been made. While Daniel prayed for his people, the angel Gabriel was sent to tell him that at the beginning of his supplication the commandment came forth. In Isaiah 65:24 it says, "Before they call, I will answer; and while they are yet speaking, I will hear." If any man still lacks faith, let him hear the words of the Lord Jesus: "Ask, and it shall be given you; seek, and ye shall find; knock, and it shall be opened unto you" (Matt. 7:7).

Of unanswered prayers we have some notable instances in the Bible. The ancient saints who prayed for the coming of the Messiah thought their prayers were of this sort. Prophets and kings desired it long, but died without the sight. Our Savior's last intercessory prayer that his followers might all be one is yet to be answered. The souls beneath the altar that have been slain for the Word of God cry for vengeance upon them that dwell upon the earth. Their cry has been put on record, but judgment is delayed. The promise of the resurrection and the life to come, of the new heaven and the new earth wherein dwelleth righteousness are among the pledged but unfulfilled assurances of prayer.

Of rejected prayers we notice first the prayers of the wicked. "If I regard iniquity in my heart, the Lord will not hear me" (Ps. 66:18). "Then shall they call upon me, but I will not answer; they shall seek me early, but they shall not find me" (Prov. 1:28). "Unto the wicked God saith, What hast thou to do to declare my statutes, or that thou shouldest take my covenant in thy mouth?" (Ps. 50:16). These prayers are rejected because of the character or purpose of the petitioner. But we also find in the Bible that some of the prayers of the saints were rejected. Where human nature cries for one thing, and the Spirit of God dictates another, it is mercy that heeds not our request. An instance of this is found in the plea of the sons of Zebedee to sit in heaven on the right and the left of the Son of man. Several times they had been the recipients of special honor. At the raising of Jairus's daughter and at the transfiguration they had been selected, with Peter and to the exclusion of the others, to accompany their Lord. Now that the kingdom of God seemed near they thought it would be a good time to make their claim. "Ye know not what ye ask. Are ye able to drink of the cup that I shall drink of, and to be baptized with the baptism that I am baptized with?" (Matt. 20:22). They said they were able, but when the time came they forsook him like the others and fled. Many times our ambitious desires are better refused. God knows what is best for us.

Again, we find one who had done much service for his Lord, praying plaintively that a thorn in the flesh might depart from him. How reasonable this appears! It was not for ambition's sake that he asked, but to remove a disability for service. It was a bodily affliction, yet so severe that he considered it a messenger of Satan sent to buffet him. Would he not be a better man without it? Three times he prayed, yet the jagged edge was thrust deeper into his side. There was no promise of removal, only the assurance, "My grace is sufficient for thee: for my strength is made perfect in weakness" (2 Cor. 12:9). How little do we know where our true gentleness lies! By suffering we are made perfect.

And lastly, there comes One who knew no sin and who had the assurance that all he had done was pleasing in the sight of his Father. "Father, if it be possible, let this cup pass from me." If atoning blood had to be shed, he was ready to shed it; but why the agonies of the cross? Three times he prays, but the answer does not come. The prayer is rejected.

And yet in all these instances may we not safely say the prayer was heard? Do not James and John sit upon thrones judging the twelve tribes of Israel? Has not the thorn long since ceased to rankle in the side of the apostle, only an honorable scar marking the place? As the maimed soldier is everywhere accorded the place of honor when the war is ended, so shall the marks of suffering in the service of Christ be the marks of distinction in the kingdom of glory. And after the resurrection we hear the risen Redeemer himself arguing from the Scriptures: "Ought not Christ to have suffered these things, and to enter into his glory?" (Luke 24:26). Suffering and glory are integral parts of redemption. The prophets prophesied of the "sufferings of Christ and the glory that should follow." The apostle argued that "we suffer with him, that we may be also glorified together."

> For it became him, for whom are all things, and by whom are all things, in bringing many sons unto glory, to make the captain of their salvation perfect through sufferings.
>
> [Hebrews 2:10]

5

Too Busy to Pray
December 27, 1890

THE surest way to kill religion is not to murder it outright but to kill it piecemeal. Neglect, more surely than the dagger, stabs religion to the heart. To give religion no set or sacred times is to murder it outright. To allow other interests, even the most pressing and benevolent, to crowd religious duties out or into a corner is to kill religion slowly but surely. A busy mother, asked how she got time to pray, replied, "I am up one hour every morning before my family stirs." This is the secret of growth in grace, of calmness and strength for the day's duties. The busy ones who have prefaced the engaging duties of the day by their hours of holy and ardent communion with God are the strong ones. Daniel was a very busy man, the cares of a great empire were on him, but he found time to pray three times every day and this praying was of more benefit to the prime minister than all his diplomacy. Christ was a very busy man. Divine business filled his heart and his hands, exhausting his time and his nerves. But Christ did not allow even God's work to crowd out his praying. Saving people from sin or suffering must not, even with Christ, be made substitutes for praying or abate in the least the time or the intensity of these holiest of seasons. He filled the day with working for God; he filled the night with praying to God. The day working made the night praying a necessity. The night praying sanctified and made successful the day working. It's true that being too busy to pray gives religion Christian burial, but it's dead, nevertheless.

Christ's Lesson in Fear
January 24, 1891

FEAR of the right kind is a mighty force. No system that proposes to affect men can afford to discard or neglect the motive of fear. It may be set aside in sentimental systems or by sentimental theorists in religion, but to those who see things as they are—who deal with verities and not with fancies, who have to work with human nature in its crude or alloy state—fear is a most valuable factor. In all sensible, practical, disciplinary systems, the motive of fear, if not the highest, is among the most powerful.

The idea that fear is the great motive in the Old Testament but that it is discredited or retired in the New may be heard in popular theology, among preachers who are on the highway of rationalism, or among a class of surface evangelists whose utterances, from a Bible point of view, must be taken with many grains of allowance.

The New Testament deals largely in the element of fear, and in a more radical, powerful, and startling way than the Old Testament. While in the New Testament the general principle of fear exists as one of the fundamental elements of piety, the fear of future punishment is awakened and matured to a vigor and authority to which the Old Testament is a stranger. The general principle of fear is referred to and enforced by a multitude of statements. The early disciples are represented as "walking in the fear of the Lord." New Testament holiness is to be perfected "in the fear of the Lord." We are charged to cover our whole Christian career with this principle and to "pass the time of our sojourning in fear" and to serve with "godly fear." In heaven they utter the cry of amazement, "Who shall not fear thee, O Lord?" And there issues from the throne the decree that is to sway heaven and earth: "Praise our God, all ye his servants, and ye that fear him." These quotations are enough to show that the New Testament neither discards nor discredits the motive of fear as an element in the purest and strongest piety.

The piety that does not have in it a strong element of fear ought to be put in a bottle to preserve it, for it will certainly evaporate, though it may be very sweet.

We have the whole matter before us in one of Christ's lessons to his disciples. He says:

> And I say unto you my friends, Be not afraid of them that kill the body, and after that have no more that they can do. But I will forewarn you whom ye shall fear: Fear him, which after he hath killed hath power to cast into hell; yea, I say unto you, Fear him.
>
> [Luke 12:4–5]

The lesson cuts two ways. It speaks against the fear of men, and strongly inculcates the fear of God. Not to fear men in a religious sense is as pious as to fear God. The two, the fear of God and the fear of men, cannot coexist. No man can truly fear God who is afraid of men. The fear of men greatly depraves the fear of God. The man-fearing spirit is as destructive to religion as is the man-pleasing spirit. To fear men is to be a coward. To fear men is to be a slave. A coward or a slave cannot serve God. The fear of men is one of the great hindrances to piety. Many have not earned the martyr's crown because they feared men. The fear of men has darkened many a radiant and cloudless experience. The fear of men tones down piety, eliminating the cross and the shame from it and destroying its savor, quenching its flame, enfeebling its vigor, sapping its life, and clothing it in attractive worldly garb, the price of its harlotry. The fear of men must go out of Christ's disciples, or his religion will go out of them.

Praying Men Wanted
February 21, 1891

PRAYER is the mightiest agent to advance God's work. Only praying hearts and hands can do God's work. Prayer succeeds when all else fails. Prayer has won great victories and rescued, with notable triumph, God's saints when every other hope was gone. Men who know how to pray are the greatest boon God can give to earth. They are the richest gift earth can offer heaven. Men who know how to use this weapon of prayer are God's best soldiers, his mightiest leaders.

Praying men are God's chosen leaders. The distinction between the leaders that God brings to the front to lead and bless his people and those leaders who owe their position of leadership to a worldly, selfish, unsanctified selection is this: God's leaders are preeminently men of prayer. Prayer distinguishes them and is the simple, divine attestation of their call, the seal of their separation by God. Whatever other graces or gifts they may have, the gift and grace of prayer towers above them all. In whatever else they may share or differ, in the gift of prayer they are one. What would God's leaders be without prayer? Strip Moses of his power in prayer, a gift that made him eminent in pagan estimate, and the crown is taken from his head, the food and fire of his faith are gone. Elijah, without his praying, would have neither record nor place in the divine legation. His life would be insipid, cowardly. Its energy, defiance, and fire gone. Without Elijah's praying, the Jordan would never have yielded to the stroke of his mantle, or would the stern angel of death have honored him with the chariot and horses of fire.

The argument that God used to quiet Ananias's fears and convince him of Paul's condition and sincerity was, "Behold, he prayeth." This was the epitome of Paul's history, the basis for his life and work. Paul, Luther, Wesley, what would these chosen ones of God be without the distinguishing and controlling element of prayer? They were leaders for God because they were mighty in prayer. They were not leaders because of their brilliance, their inexhaustible resources, their magnificent cultured or native endowment. They were leaders because they could command the power of God by the power of prayer. Praying men are not just men who say prayers or men who pray by habit. Praying men are men with whom prayer is a mighty force, an energy that moves heaven and pours untold treasures of good on earth.

Praying men are the men who spend much time with God. Praying men always feel a great need and desire to be alone with God. Though very busy men, they always stop at some appointed time for communion with God. They have spent much time alone with him and have found that the secret of wise and powerful leadership for God is in these seasons of special access and grace. Praying men are the men of the single eye. They have been so much alone with God, have seen so much of his glory, have learned so much of his will, have been fashioned so strongly after his image that he fixes and fills their gaze. All else is too insignificant to engage their attention, too little to catch their eye. A double vision—one for self, and the other for God—mightily hinders prayer. Praying men are men of one book; they feed on God's Word; it lives in them in vitalizing force and abides in them in full authority and faith. They are Bible men. The Bible inspires their prayers and quickens their faith. They rest on its promises as on a globe of granite.

Praying men are the only productive workers for God. True prayer is a working force, a divine energy that must come out, that is too strong to be still. The work of praying men achieves the best results because it is done by God's energy. Praying men have his direction and do his work for his glory, under the full and cheering beam of his presence, his Word, and his Spirit.

Praying men serve to protect the church from the materialism that affects all its plans and polity and hardens its lifeblood. A secret, deadly poison circulates, convincing the church that it need not be so dependent on purely spiritual forces as it used to be. Changed times and changed conditions have brought it out of its spiritual straits and dependencies and put it where other forces can bear it to its climax. A fatal snare of this kind has lured the church into worldly embraces, dazzled her leaders, weakened her foundations, and deprived her of much of her beauty and strength. Praying men save the church from this material tendency. They pour into it the original spiritual forces. They lift it from the sandbars of materialism and press it out into the ocean depths of spiritual power. Praying men keep God in the church in full force. They keep his hand on the helm as he trains the church in strength and trust.

The number and efficiency of the laborers in God's vineyard in all lands is dependent on the men of prayer. By the divinely arranged process, the number and success of the consecrated laborers depend on the power of prayer. Prayer opens wide the doors of access, prepares the laborer to enter, and gives holy boldness, firmness, and fruit. Praying men are needed in all fields of spiritual labor. There is no position, high or low, in the church of God that can be well filled without prayer. There is no position where Christians are found that does not demand a faith that always prays and never faints. Praying men are needed in the house of business as well as in the house of God that they may order and direct trade, not according to the maxims of this world, but according to Bible precepts and the maxims of the heavenly life.

Men of prayer are needed especially in the positions of church influence, honor, and power. The leaders of church thought, church work, and church life should be men of signal power in prayer. It is the praying heart that sanctifies the toil and skill of the hands and the toil and wisdom of the head. Prayer keeps work aligned with God's will and keeps thought aligned with God's Word. The solemn responsibilities of leadership in God's church, in a large or limited sphere, should be so hedged about with prayer that between it and the world there would be an impassable gulf. Leaders should be so elevated and purified by prayer that neither cloud nor night would stain the radiance or dim the sight of a constant meridian view of God. Many church leaders seem to think that if they can be prominent as men of thought, of plans, of scholarly attainments, of eloquent gifts, and conspicuous activities, that these are enough and will atone for the absence of the higher spiritual power that comes from much prayer. But these are vain and paltry in the serious work of bringing glory to God, controlling the church for him, and bringing it into full accord with its divine mission.

Praying men are the men who have done so much for God in the past. They are the ones who have won the victories for God and spoiled his foes. They are the ones who have set up his kingdom in the very camps of his enemies. There are no other conditions for success today. The nineteenth century has not suspended the necessity or force of prayer. There is no substitute by which its gracious ends can be secured. Only praying hands can build for God. Men of prayer are God's mighty ones on earth, his master builders. They may be destitute of all else, but with the wrestlings and prevailings of a simple-hearted faith they are mighty—the mightiest for God. Church leaders may be gifted in all else, but without this greatest of gifts they are as Samson shorn of his locks, or as the altars of the temple where heavenly flame has died without the divine presence.

The Wrath of God

July 25, 1891

THE idea that God is a God of justice, a God whose indignation flames against evil and evildoers, is an idea that the present age is not inclined to tolerate. We must have a God according to our notions. He must be fashioned in agreement with our lusts. We make him like us.

Our diminished estimation of God's nature is an evil of great magnitude. It effaces our conception of sin and destroys our sensitivity to right and wrong. We begin to think that God is indifferent to the distinctions between sin and holiness. We begin to question God's wrath towards the sinner. Should we then make distinctions that God does not recognize? Should we condemn things that God does not condemn? These errors and others come from the fact that we do not make the Bible our authority. Too often our theories are formed by our desires, our need to cover our sins, our false views of God's nature, or our partial views of his word. God's wrath and God's punishment go together. God is not a cold being without feeling who punishes by the icy deliverances of a law—a mere machine in the hands of his own laws—but he feels as well as punishes. He flames with indignation as well as decrees with authority.

His anger is the fire that burns. The mightiest being in the universe is God, and his feelings the most profound.

We do not propose here to make an exhaustive presentation of New Testament teaching on this subject but will confine our statements to two points of view. The first will be that of John the Baptist, whose system was introductory to and merged in that of Christ's. If the Old Testament idea of God's hatred of sin, his inflexible opposition to it, and his purpose to punish it is to be retired, or reversed, or in any way discounted, then this change in God's nature, plan, and principles will be evident either in direct statements from the honest and fearless Baptist or in his fixed silence.

John the Baptist has no new God to proclaim, no new revelation to make. He draws no invidious comparisons between the Old and the New Testaments, such as are so familiar in modern religious thought. It never occurred to him to contrast the two to the detriment of the Old. He joins the two, showing that the New, by its trueness to the Old, was heaven's appointed successor to the Old.

> Then said he to the multitude that came forth to be baptized of him, O generation of vipers, who hath warned you to flee from the wrath to come?
>
> [Luke 3:7]

> And now also the axe is laid unto the root of the trees: every tree therefore which bringeth not forth good fruit is hewn down, and cast into the fire.
>
> [Luke 3:9]

> I indeed baptize you with water unto repentance: but he that cometh after me is mightier than I, whose shoes I am not worthy to bear: he shall baptize you with the Holy Ghost, and with fire: whose fan is in his hand, and he will thoroughly purge his floor, and gather his wheat into the garner; but he will burn up the chaff with unquenchable fire.
>
> [Matthew 3:11, 12]

This is the way he preaches, prophesies, and announces Christ, by projecting the fiery, searching, penal elements of the old dispensation into the new. In the last verse of the third chapter of John, the Baptist presents the full import of gospel statements and conditions. "He that believeth on the Son hath everlasting life: and he that believeth not the Son shall not see life; but the wrath of God abideth on him." This is the announcement of perpetual conditions and results. The wrath of God now abides on the unbeliever. The penalty of violated law will be exacted after a while, but the wrath is a present, existing thing. God is angry at the sinner every day and always. John the Baptist has announced that under the gospel this is the attitude of God towards sinners.

We will view this doctrine as presented in the Book of Revelation by one greater than the Baptist—John, the beloved disciple—and see if these closing pictures illustrate a different gospel. It must be borne in mind that this Book of Revelation came through John, the very synonym of love, the one of all the Twelve the nearest to Christ's person and the nearest his character, the best loved.

He was chosen to close God's revelation to man in a book that clothes Christ with all the plenitude of penal justice. This John with all his tenderness puts God in the unfolding history of the church up to its close in most thorough accord with all antecedent revelation and in the sweetest harmony with the character and teaching of Christ. There are in this revelation no sentimental strains from which the rod, the fire, the law, and the punishment are unceremoniously dismissed as the crude or savage ministers of a crude or savage state. We have this picture:

> And the third angel followed them, saying with a loud voice, If any man worship the beast and his image, and receive his mark in his forehead, or in his hand, the same shall drink of the wine of the wrath of God, which is poured out without mixture into the cup of his indignation; and he shall be tormented with fire and brim-

stone in the presence of the holy angels, and in the presence of the
Lamb: and the smoke of their torment ascendeth up for ever and
ever: and they have no rest day nor night, who worship the beast
and his image, and whosoever receiveth the mark of his name. . . .
And the angel thrust in his sickle into the earth, and gathered the
vine of the earth, and cast it into the great winepress of the wrath
of God.

[Revelation 14:9–11, 19]

Again, the Revelation says,

And I saw another sign in heaven, great and marvelous, seven angels
having the seven last plagues; for in them is filled up the wrath of
God.

[Revelation 15:1]

And the command was given them:

And I heard a great voice out of the temple saying to the seven angels,
Go your ways, and pour out the vials of the wrath of God upon the
earth.

[Revelation 16:1]

Of Christ as he goes forth to establish his kingdom with conquering power, it is said,

And out of his mouth goeth a sharp sword, that with it he should
smite the nations, and he shall rule them with a rod of iron, and he
treadeth the winepress of the fierceness and wrath of Almighty God.

[Revelation 19:15]

Of Christ, in his closing up of this dispensation, the most
terrific description is given of his wrath:

And the kings of the earth, and the great men, and the rich men, and
the chief captains, and the mighty men, and every bondman, and
every free man, hid themselves in the dens and in the rocks of the
mountains; and said to the mountains and rocks, Fall on us, and hide
us from the face of him that sitteth on the throne, and from the wrath

of the Lamb: for the great day of his wrath is come; and who shall be able to stand?

[Revelation 6:15–17]

We have this description of lost characters and their fearful doom:

But the fearful, and unbelieving, and the abominable and murderers, and whoremongers, and sorcerers, and idolators, and all liars, shall have their part in the lake which burneth with fire and brimstone; which is the second death.

[Revelation 21:8]

John continues his appalling pictures of God's wrath coming out in the events of world history and in the direct infliction of penalty as the result of the decisions of the day of judgment. As a result of the searching scrutiny of that day John says, "Whosoever was not found written in the book of life was cast into the lake of fire."

John ends the magnificent description of the glorious city of our God by closing its pearly gates and barring access to the disobedient with these words:

And there shall in no wise enter into it any thing that defileth, neither whatsoever worketh abomination, or maketh a lie: but they which are written in the Lamb's book of life.

[Revelation 21:27]

Modern advocates of what is termed the gospel of love have another gospel than that which John, the true advocate of the true gospel of love, had.

The opening of Christ's dispensation by John the Baptist with all the sternness of the reformer and all the severity of law and the closing of that dispensation by John the beloved disciple with all the fiery indignation and faithful severity of true love come to the same point. They blend the two elements in God's nature, which are never to be separated: our God is love and our God is a consuming fire. This dual being is one. His mercy and justice conspire to the same ends. His dispensations are one. It could not be otherwise while God is God, while law is law, while sin is sin. It could not be otherwise if holiness and heaven are to be secured and perpetuated.

Wrestling Prayer
August 15, 1891

PRAYER in its highest and most availing form is accomplished with the attitude of wrestling with God. It is the contest and victory of faith, a victory not secured from an enemy but from one who tries our faith that he may enlarge and increase its desires. He makes the acquisition of great spiritual good a notable event in our experience, a transitional epoch with which a new spiritual calendar may begin. The Bible makes it clear that there are unseen and malign forces that array themselves to resist the soul's highest and strongest approaches to God. These forces will bring disaster to all feeble efforts to secure from God the full measure of the soul's gracious inheritance.

The wrestler, in Bible figure, who in close contact expends great effort, symbolizes the intense spiritual energy that attends the highest form of prayer. It is the attitude of a soul humbled by a great need, impassioned by a great desire, energized and sustained by the knowledge that only by wrestling with God in prayer can he gain and more than gain the realization of the most ardent spiritual desires. The Bible is inexhaustible in its illustration of the fact that the highest spiritual good is secured from the highest form of spiritual effort. Grace it is, but grace in its rewarding, compensating form. There is no room in the plans of grace for feeble desires, listless efforts, lazy attitudes. All must be ardent, vigorous, vigilant. Inflamed desires and impassioned efforts delight heaven. God would have his children be in dead earnest about the things of eternity. He does not tolerate halfheartedness and has only indignation and disgust for timorous dealing, indecision, and lukewarmness.

Isaiah laments that there was no one who stirred himself up to take hold of God. Much praying was done, but it was too easy, indifferent, complacent. There were no mighty movements of the soul toward God, no array of all the sanctified energies to reach and grapple with God and draw out his treasures for spiritual uses. Forceless prayers have no power to overcome difficulties, no power to win marked results or gain a complete and wonderful victory.

The prophet looks forward with hopeful eye to the future, when religion would flourish and there would be times of real praying. The watchmen would not abate their vigilance or crying day or night. Their urgent, persistent efforts were to keep all spiritual interests excited and draw continually from God's inexhaustible treasures. With a kind of surprised emphasis and a commanding authority, God chides our timid prayers. "Ask me," he says, "of things to come concerning my sons, and concerning the work of my hands command ye me" (Isa. 45:11). He hereby puts himself in our hands and gives up his keys to the authority of an all-conquering faith. This gracious attitude of God is to create and mature in us the forces of resistless praying, forces that must underlie the praying that reaches and affects the destiny of things.

Jacob is an illustration for all time of the commanding and conquering forces in prayer—the strength of weakness, the power of self-despair, the energy of perseverance, the elevation of humility, the victory of surrender. Jacob's salvation issued from the forces that he massed in that all-night conflict.

The decree for Hezekiah's death had been issued, and Isaiah was commissioned to inform him of God's purposes and charge him to get ready at once. Hezekiah desired to live, but what can change God's decree? Nothing but the energy of faith. Hezekiah's heart was broken under the strain, and its waters flowed and added force and volume to his praying. He pleaded with great strivings and with strong arguments; and God heard Hezekiah praying, saw his tears, and changed his mind. Hezekiah lived to praise God and to be an example of the power of mighty praying.

Decent, shallow praying did not suit Paul. He puts himself in the attitude of a wrestler and charges his brethren to join him in the agony of a great conflict. "Brethren, I beseech you," he says, "for the Lord Jesus Christ's sake, and for the love of the Spirit, that ye strive together with me in your prayers" (Rom. 15:30). He was too much in earnest to treat praying with gloved hands. In it he agonized, and he desired his brethren to be his partners in this conflict and wrestling of his soul. Epaphras was doing this same kind of praying for the Colossians: "always laboring fervently for you in prayers, that ye may stand perfect and complete in all the will of God." This is an end worth agonizing over. One source of the purity and power of the church was this kind of praying by these early pastors.

Prayer, to be efficient, must have life. It must be living. It must be energized by all the forces that can be kindled in the soul by a great faith, a great need, and a great desire. "The effectual fervent prayer of a righteous man availeth much" (James 5:16). The energy of the prayer comes from all these forces of the righteous man, and all the latent vigor of the soul is aroused and kindled by the inner power and fire of the Holy Ghost. Elijah is the embodiment and example of the full, true play of these forces.

The Syrophoenician woman's prayer is an example of divine wrestling and conflict more real and involving more vital energy and endurance than was ever illustrated in the conflicts of Isthmia or Olympia.

Christ's life flowed through his praying. "Who in the days of his flesh offered up prayers and supplications with strong crying and tears" (Heb. 5:7). Everything yielded to the impetuous current of his prayers. Nature stood still or moved on in silence as he prayed all night; the transfiguring glory of heaven, its chief inhabitants, angels, and men stood ready and eager to do the bidding of his resistless praying.

Christ teaches by command and precept the idea of energy and earnestness in praying. He gives to our efforts gradation and climax. We are to ask, but to the asking we must add seeking, and seeking must pass into the full effort of knocking. God's silence arouses the pleading soul to greater effort. Denial, instead of abating or abasing the desire, must arouse the soul's latent energies and kindle anew its highest ardor.

Our praying may be sincere, but it may be only half in earnest. It lacks the fire and sustained energy that gives delight to heaven and secures the largest and richest measure of good. We are poor indeed because our prayers expose and add to our poverty. Many people mouth prayers. Others pray to be heard by men. Rare indeed are the prayers that move God mightily and stir into concern and activity all the forces of heaven. Praying is too often the result of a decent performance, a professional demand, or a matter of habit. Our prayers do not come from burdened souls and are not born in the fire of a great desire and pursued through the deepest agony of conflict and opposition. Our spiritual cravings are not strong enough to give life to the mighty conflicts of prayer. They are not absorbing enough to stop business, arrest worldly pursuits, awaken us before day, and send us to the closet, to solitude, and to God in order to conquer every opposing force and win our victories from the very jaws of hell. Men and women are needed who can exploit the uses, the forces, the blessing, and the utmost limits of prayer.

10

Fire
September 12, 1891

FIRE is a symbol for God. "Our God," said the apostle, "is a consuming fire." His appearance to Moses was in the burning bush. Sinai glowed and burned and trembled at his presence. The pillar of fire was the signal of his directing care over Israel. The fire in the tabernacle and temple proclaimed his favor and was the perpetual symbol of his presence. Christ came to baptize with fire as well as the Holy Ghost, and his second coming will be in flaming fire. Pentecost, with its tongues of fire, symbolized the ardency and flame with which the new dispensation was to be made universal. This baptism of fire on the day of Pentecost brought the dispensation of the Spirit into harmony with the past dispensations and made fire the radical symbol of divine energy, which is to characterize these last days. Because fire searches and purifies, it symbolizes that energy, which is the efficient force in religion, whether in individual or church life.

Zeal is a contagious, but not a popular, element. Our fathers took their tea piping hot; we take ours iced. Iced religion is more popular and tasteful than iced tea. We can endure in our religion enough warmth to take the chill off, but more than this is offensive. We have added many good elements to our preaching, but these cannot make up for the loss of fervor. The average mind can only be moved to action by a flame. Some men may pull through to heaven on a cold collar, but they are the exception. A Scotsman is the last man we would expect to criticize us for our lack of fire. A Scottish doctor of divinity, writing of his trip to this country, says,

> I spent ten Sabbaths in the United States and during all of these (as I was forbidden to preach) I was a listener. It may have been my misfortune, but it is the fact, that nowhere did I light upon an overflowing congregation; nor did I hear, except once (in a Methodist church) any sermon delivered with extraordinary fervor. Again and again did we come upon respectable congregations, in which there were angry appearances of devoutness and earnestness, and the sermons we heard were always excellent. But there was no fire sensible (and it may have been our fault), but we came and went without ever being greatly stirred. It is more than likely that if an American traveler were to journey through Scotland in the like way, he would have a similar experience, but I am now speaking only of my own experience and it may do good and not harm to state it. Certainly ministers alike with you and with us need to be reminded how much the life of the church depends upon the fervor of their preaching.

A dwindling flame destroys the vital and aggressive forces in church life. God must be represented by a fiery church or he is not truly represented. God is all on fire, and his church, if it be like him, must also be aflame with the great and eternal interests of religion. Zeal need not be fussy to be consuming and forceful. Christ was as far removed as possible from nervous excitability, the very opposite of intolerant or clamorous zeal, and yet the zeal of God's house consumed him. The world is feeling his fierce flame and responding to it with an ever-increasing readiness and an ever-enlarging circle.

The lack of ardor in Christian profession or action is a sure sign of the want of depth and intensity. The lack of fire is the sure sign of the lack of God's presence. To abate fervor is to retire God. God can tolerate many things in the way of infirmity or error. He can pardon much when one is penitent, but two things are intolerable to him, insincerity and lukewarmness. Lack of heart and lack of heat are the things that he loathes. "I would thou wert cold or hot. So then because thou art luke- warm, and neither cold nor hot, I will spew thee out of my mouth," is God's judgment on the lack of fire in the Christian church and in Christian character. Fire is the motor that moves religion. Religious principles that are not aflame have neither force nor perfume. Flame is the wing by which faith ascends, and fervency is the soul of prayer. Love is kindled in a flame, and flame is the air that religion breathes. It feeds on fire. Religion can stand anything better than a feeble flame.

Christian character needs to be set on fire. Lack of heat makes more infidels than lack of faith. Not to be in fiery earnest about the things of heaven is not to be about them at all. The fiery souls are the ones that win in the heavenly fight. Nothing short of red hot can keep the glow of heaven in these chilly climes. We must grasp the live coal and covet the consuming flame. We are getting low in our spiritual temperature when we freeze a Scotsman out.

How the Revival Begins
December 19, 1891

THE revival begins in prayer. The prayerful spirit is the spirit of the revival. The spirit of supplicating prayer is the pledge of the revival, its harbinger and source. The revival begins in prayer, continues by prayer, and if it ends well, ends in prayer.

Mr. Finney, the great revivalist, relates that in a certain town there had been no revival for many years. The church was nearly run out. The people were unconverted. Spiritual desolation reigned. There lived in the town an old blacksmith who stammered so greatly that it was painful to hear him speak. At work in his shop his mind became greatly exercised about the church; his agony was so great he locked the door and spent the afternoon in prayer, prevailing with God. He then obtained the reluctant consent of his pastor to plan a meeting. The preacher had no hope of any attendance, but the room filled to overflowing. All was silent for a time until one sinner broke out in tears and begged for someone to pray for him. Others followed, and it was found that people from every quarter of the town were under deep conviction. All dated their conviction from the hour the old man was praying in his shop. A powerful revival followed. This old, stammering man prevailed and, as a prince, had power with God.

Several members of Jonathan Edwards's church had spent the whole night in prayer before he preached his memorable sermon, "Sinners in the Hands of an Angry God." The Holy Ghost was so mightily poured out, and God so manifest in his majesty and holiness during the preaching of that sermon, that the elders threw their arms around the pillars of the church and cried, "Lord save us; we are slipping down to hell."

The revival begins always in mighty prayer. The number praying may be few. The pastor alone may be carrying the burden of a broken heart and crying to God in his penitence, sighs, and tears. The praying ones may be a small circle, but whether the praying ones be the pastor or people, the circle of prayer is always the center of the revival. It begins with the praying ones. The ones who stir themselves up to take hold of God are the human sources of the revival. Many of our meetings seem to be planned as substitutes for prayer. It is much easier to send for a reputed evangelist to stir up a revival than to pray fervently and long until revival happens. It is much easier to engineer a great religious movement by human forces than it is to break our hearts and humble ourselves in the dust before God that he may inaugurate a real religious movement. It is much easier to get up a summer Chautauqua and preach about saving the heathen than it is to place ourselves in their stead, as their substitutes before God, and plead with him until he touches, overpowers, and influences all the springs of human and divine action and gives us "the heathen for thine inheritance, and the uttermost parts of the earth for thy possession."

 The spirit of prayer cannot be in harmony with the spirit of entertainment in the church of God. If every Southern Methodist church would discard the entertainment business, cease making God's house a house of merchandise, make his house the house of prayer, and commit itself in penitent earnestness to importunate and prevailing prayer, our revival stream would run ocean floods and all our churches would be aflame with God's glory and resonant with his praises and the Lord would add daily to our churches thousands of the saved. Then the beauty of the Lord our God would be upon us, and he would establish the work of our hands.

Pentecost's Lessons
December 26, 1891

WHAT is Pentecost? Is it an historic fact only—fossilized, barren, past? Or is it a present, living energy that should be reproduced in the history of every individual and every church in all places and for all times? Pentecost is but the gospel in practical and full operation. Pentecost is but the Holy Ghost in concrete form. Pentecost gives the power that executes the gospel. The gospel cannot be carried out in any place or under any conditions in an aggressive, authoritative way without pentecostal power. What the Holy Ghost was to the disciples on the day of Pentecost he must be to us. The Holy Ghost set the church in motion with full force, and he alone can keep the church moving and empowered.

The fullness of spiritual life is one of the most evident and most remarkable features of Pentecost. The spiritual life of Pentecost is conscious, happy, overflowing and floods individuals and the church so that meetings are exuberant and inspiring. Deadness, dumbness, and dryness seem forever banished. The fullness of the God-life impregnates and quickens. The richness and opulence of the spiritual life creates an ecstasy that seems to outsiders a senseless, noisy delirium or the intoxication of new wine. It is the new wine of the kingdom. The waters of that stream that makes glad the city of our God have burst in upon our desert world, bringing richness and joy. The inner life is at floodtide.

This is the first lesson of Pentecost for us, that the spiritual life can be full of joy and power. When the spiritual life is feeble, uncertain, faint; when doubts disturb or becloud or joy is dead, we know that the Holy Ghost is not there in power, if there at all. His presence illumines and gladdens like the glorious rising of the sun. We may substitute a thousand things for the Holy Ghost and delude ourselves by fancying that these substitutes are life-giving forces, but then we will never know the power and life of Pentecost.

Pentecost teaches us about activity, activity that flows from the internal life and is full of strength. This activity is not forced, not induced by outward pressure. Holy Ghost life cannot be inactive; it must express itself in doing good. Its activities are spontaneous and irresistible. True spiritual life can no more cease to work than the sun can cease to shine. To minister is the condition of this life. It is the same life that inspired him who went about doing good. As long as good is done, the life remains, but the life and the title are surrendered when the commitment to work fails.

This activity is not generated by the rush and heat of young blood, the desire to be noticed, or the pride of leadership. A strong, sweet force from within—as prevalent and potent as gravity—demands and directs this activity. Its law is lowly service, humble as the seraphim—who veils its feet as well as its face—and as fiery and adoring.

Pentecost has its lesson of organization and order. Its organization is simple and complete, with the Holy Ghost in sovereign authority, placing every member in order and in due subordination. Like the members of the human body and made by the same divine hand, each member of the spiritual body has its place and function.

The sovereign sway and fullness of the Holy Ghost in the church destroys all envy, ambition, and schism in the body and qualifies each member to discharge his function.

> From whom the whole body fitly joined together and compacted by that which every joint supplieth, according to the effectual working in the measure of every part, maketh increase of the body unto the edifying of itself in love.
>
> [Ephesians 4:16]

This is not an organization created by the skill of an ecclesiastical legislator but a compact and complete organization formed by the Holy Ghost within. The Holy Ghost organizes the man within in harmony with the divine will that he may do God's work with ease and perfection. The Holy Ghost, not more machinery, is what the church needs, for he enables the individual member to take his place in the body and perform his divinely appointed functions. The great bane and weakness of the church is to run on natural and material forces, to engineer and execute its work with human and social forces and not Holy Ghost power. Organization cannot give life or restore it. The most skillful array and arrangement of church or material forces will not give life or increase it. The day after Pentecost the church was complete as a spiritual organization, as if it had been growing for centuries. This was not the result of legislation or growth, but it was the result of the presence and fullness of the Holy Ghost.

Pentecost made a witnessing church. Before Pentecost the disciples had the facts, but they could not project them with convicting force. Pentecost took the facts of history and observation and put them as a divinely vitalized force into their hearts. It was a new era as well as a new energy for them—a new dispensation, not divorced from the past but married to it by stronger ties. Pentecost not only embellished and illumined the past but encompassed it in the more excellent glory of the present.

The tongues of fire are the symbol of the most important function of the church: witness. The tongues of fire also symbolize the one energy needed for that witness: the fire of the Holy Ghost. The tongue of fire tells with fiery, searching energy the truths that the Holy Ghost has impassioned. Witnessing must be forceful and carry conviction. Our word "martyr" means witness and signifies those who have a death-hold on the truth of God, those into whom the truth of God has gone with a force that presses itself in strong, earnest convictions and statements. Men and women who declare always and at any cost the hope that is in them are witnesses. None but a Holy Ghost church can witness. Holy Ghost Christians always witness. A Holy Ghost church is a verbal church. Praises, prayer, and testimony are as native to such a church as to heaven, after which the true church was patterned.

Pentecost teaches us about simplicity, unity, and brotherliness. They were one, "eating their meat with gladness and singleness of heart." They were united in a strong and happy brotherhood—a fellowship that made them partners. The factitious, illusive, and separating conditions of society were destroyed. The bond of grace was stronger than caste, society, or blood. Ambition and worldliness, the source of discontent and agitation, were gone. The Holy Ghost had cured these chronic sins. The disintegrating elements that divorce men were removed in the interests of a holy brotherhood. The clamor, selfishness, and severity of personal rights were gladly relinquished for the furtherance of this new fraternity. This brotherhood, with its simplicity and oneness, is very different from social ties, which have been so generally substituted for it. These social ties, created by church members, ecclesiastical drill, or worldly manipulations and motives are very feeble, often hollow, and always local. They may be nonspiritual in nature and worldly in their tendency, taste, and ties. The Holy Ghost creates a brotherhood of sympathy and love that is spiritual and mighty in its assertions, and heaven-directed in all its tendencies. It removes the false distinctions, which society, money, or place have created, and unites the rich and poor and the high and the low in a holy commune from which selfishness, envy, and pride are forever excluded.

Pentecost solved the money question. The church has more trouble with money than with anything else. Money secularizes the church, depleting its spirituality and heavenliness. Money arrests liberal giving; the more we have, as a general thing, the less we give. It steals the heart of the pew from heaven, and it enters the pulpit, which is often busier and heartier about money-making than it is about soul-saving. Pentecost, for that time, solved the money problem because it broke up selfishness, its source, root, and branch. The early Christians sold their real estate and laid the money at the apostles' feet to be used for God and for the purposes of this holy brotherhood. The record is complete:

> The multitude of them that believed were of one heart and of one soul: neither said any of them that aught of the things which he possessed was his own; but they had all things common. . . . Neither was there any among them that lacked: for as many as were possessors of lands or houses sold them, and brought the prices of the things that were sold, and laid them down at the apostles' feet: and distribution was made unto every man according as he had need.
>
> [Acts 4:32, 34–35]

The Holy Ghost in the fullness of his power is the only remedy for the cancer of covetousness, which has fastened itself with deadly force on our spiritual vitals. The power of the Holy Ghost is the only force that can fill our depleted treasury and bring Christian giving up to where the law of Christian self-denial dictates, up to liberal Christian giving, which is our responsibility.

Pentecost has its lessons on drawing a crowd, reaching the masses, church influence, and church attraction. At Pentecost, the people were drawn, convicted, and saved. The populace feared the church and favored the church. The saved were drawn to it. A church with Holy Ghost fire, Holy Ghost organi-

zation, and Holy Ghost brotherhood solves these modern questions of drawing people and reaching the masses, for it is a live,
active, and aggressive church.

Pentecost teaches the pulpit about courage and transforming
power. Peter had preached before, but the fire of Pentecost both
burned up his old sermons and gave him new ones. The fire
gave us a new Peter. Where is the pulpit or the church that does
not need a new Pentecost? Where is the pulpit, where is the
church, that is waiting for this baptism of fire as the apostles
waited for it in supplication and in prayer with one accord and
in one place?

13

A Prayerful Ministry
February 18, 1892

GOD'S true preachers have been distinguished by one feature, they have been men of prayer. Differing often in many things, they have always had a common center. They may have started from different points and traveled different roads, but they converged to one point. They were one in prayer. To them God was the center of attraction, and prayer the path that led to God. These men prayed not occasionally, not a little at regular or at odd times, but they so prayed that it entered into and shaped their characters. They so prayed as to affect their own lives and the lives of others. They so prayed as to make the history of the church and influence the current of the times. They spent so much time in prayer, not because they marked the shadow on the dial or the hands on the clock, but because it was to them so momentous and engaging a business that they could scarcely give it up.

Prayer was to them what it was to Paul, a striving with earnest effort of soul; what it was to Jacob, a wrestling and a prevailing; what it was to Christ, "strong crying and tears." They prayed "always with all prayer and supplication in the Spirit, and watching thereunto with all perseverance." "The effectual fervent prayer" has been the mightiest weapon of

God's mightiest soldiers. Elijah, who was a man subject to like passions as we are, prayed earnestly that it might not rain. And it did not rain on earth for three years and six months. And he prayed again, and the heaven gave rain, and the earth brought forth her fruit. Elijah is like all prophets and preachers who have moved their generations for God, and he used the same instrument by which they all worked their wonders.

Prayer is not a little habit pinned on to us while we were tied to our mother's apron strings, and it isn't a little quarter-of-a-minute's grace said over an hour's dinner, but it is a most serious work of our most serious years. It must engage more of time and appetite than our longest dinings or richest feasts.

The prayer that makes much of our preaching must be made much of. The character of our praying will determine the character of our preaching. Light praying will make light preaching. Prayer makes preaching strong, gives it unction, and makes it stick. In every ministry weighty for good, prayer has always been a serious business. Paul's declaration "night and day praying exceedingly" is a condensed record of the engrossing nature of prayer to an apostolic man. His solemn charge to the Roman Christians, "Now I beseech you, brethren, for the Lord Jesus Christ's sake, and for the love of the Spirit, that ye strive together with me in your prayers to God for me," shows how important this matter of prayer was in his estimate and ministry, and how to him it was an agony of earnest striving to God. The summary that he makes of the ministry of Epaphras as "laboring fervently for you in prayers" puts prayer as the most important part of the preacher's machinery. Christ's life in the flesh is reduced to a verse of prayer statistics:

> Who in the days of his flesh, when he had offered up prayers and supplications with strong crying and tears unto him that was able to save him from death, and was heard in that he feared.
>
> [Hebrews 5:7]

The necessity and importance of prayer to Christ is emphasized by his practice. "And in the morning, rising up a great while before day, he went out, and departed into a solitary place, and there prayed" (Mark 1:35). This shows us how he denied himself in the interest of prayer, how he suspended sleep in the interests of real praying. We have the record, "He went out into a mountain to pray, and continued all night in prayer to God." We don't know how many unrecorded instances of this kind marked his life. His teaching as well as his example emphasized prayer: "He spake a parable unto them to this end, that men ought always to pray, and not to faint."

The apostles knew the necessity and worth of prayer to their ministry. They knew that their high commission as apostles, instead of relieving them from the necessity of prayer, committed them to it by a more urgent need. They were exceedingly jealous else some other important work should exhaust their time and prevent them from·praying as they ought, so they appointed laymen to look after the delicate and engrossing duties of ministering to the poor that they, the apostles, might give themselves "continually to prayer, and to the ministry of the word." Prayer comes first. They surrender themselves to prayer, putting fervor, urgency, perseverance, and time into it.

The praying that makes a powerful ministry is not like an herb added to the pot for flavor, but it is an integral part of the stew. Praying comes from within the body, as much a part of it as the blood and bones. Prayer is no petty duty put into a corner, no piecemeal performance made out of the fragments of time that have been snatched from business and other engagements of life. Prayer takes the best of time. The heart of our time and strength must be given to it. It does not mean going to the prayer closet after we have become absorbed in the study or swallowed up in the activities of ministerial duties, but it means going to the closet first and putting the study and activities second. Both study and activities are freshened and made efficient by the closet. Prayer that affects one's ministry must give tone to one's life. The praying that gives color and beat to character is no pleasant hurried pastime. It must enter as strongly into the heart and life as Christ's "strong crying and tears" did, must draw out the soul into an agony of desire as Paul's did, must be an inner fire and force like the "effectual fervent prayer" of James, must be of the quality that reaches God and works mighty spiritual revolutions.

It is a spiritual axiom that in every truly successful ministry prayer is an evident and controlling force—evident and controlling in the life of the preacher, evident and controlling in the deep spirituality of his work. A ministry may be a very thoughtful ministry without prayer; the preacher may secure fame and popularity without prayer; the whole machinery of the preacher's life and work may be run without the oil of prayer, or with scarcely enough to grease one cog; but no ministry can be a spiritual one, securing holiness in the preacher and in his people, without prayer being made an evident and controlling force.

The preacher that prays indeed puts God into the work. God does not come into the preacher's work as a matter of course, or on general principles, but he comes by prayer and special urgency. That God will be with us when we seek him with the whole heart is as true of the preacher as of the penitent. A prayerful ministry is the only ministry that brings the preacher into sympathy with the people. Prayer unites us with the human as much as it unites us with the divine. A prayerful ministry is the only ministry qualified for the high offices and responsibilities of the preacher. Colleges, books, theology, and preaching do not make a preacher, but praying does. The apostles' commission to preach was a blank till that was filled only by the Pentecost, which praying brought. A prayerful ministry has passed beyond the regions of the popular and the mundane, beyond ecclesiastical organization and into a sublimer and mightier region, the region of the spiritual, where holiness is the product of the work, and transfigured hearts and lives emblazon the reality of the work, revealing its true and substantial nature. God is with this preacher. His ministry is not based on worldly or surface principles. He has been deeply schooled in and has deeply stored the things of God. His deep communion with God about his people and the agony of his wrestling spirit have crowned him a prince in the things of God. The iciness of the mere professional has long since melted under the intensity of his praying.

The superficial results of many a ministry and the deadness of still other ministries can be traced to the lack of praying. Prayer must be fundamental, ever abiding, ever increasing. The text and the sermon should be the result of prayer. The study should be bathed in prayer; all its duties impregnated with prayer; its whole spirit the spirit of prayer. "I am sorry that I have prayed so little" was the deathbed regret of one of God's chosen ones—a sad and remorseful regret for a preacher. "I want a life of greater, deeper, truer prayer," said the late Archbishop Tait. So may we all say, and this may we all secure.

14

Time and Place for Prayer
March 24, 1892

TIME and place, though they do not belong to the very essence of prayer, are conditions that are essential to its true performance and best results. Favorable conditions are absolutely necessary if great enterprises and solemn duties are not to be maimed or miscarried. Prayer has many forms of expression, but there must be time and place for uninterrupted secret prayer or all the varied forms of expression will cease or will become cold, listless, or fruitless.

Prayer is the audience that God gives to man, and to have no place consecrated to such an audience and no time set apart as sacred to this divine communion, is to treat with contempt the audience and all its important interests and to treat with indignity the majestic being who condescends to so highly privilege us. The time for such blessed communion must not be left to chance or to the hurried moments that may be snatched from other engagements. That which is worth doing at all is worth doing well. To set aside no time for prayer is not to pray at all. To have no place to pray is to make prayer an airy, impalpable thing. Prayer is the Christian's responsible office. The official position he holds is that of intercessor. The Christian is God's priest, and to give neither time nor place to the holy duties of this office is to forfeit it. Prayer is the Christian's great business, and to give neither time nor place to the praying business is nothing more nor less than shameful bankruptcy. The only way to make the business of praying successful is to enter into it in a diligent and earnest way, meeting all the conditions that tend to make it successful.

The reason why so little praying is done, and why the little praying that is done secures so few and feeble results, is that the conditions of time and place are not met. Those who are careful to arrange the conditions of time and space for prayer are the ones who secure the greatest results and to whom prayer becomes more and more potent and attractive. The history of religion will not afford an example of one who has been a powerful spiritual factor in the church who has not been noted for prayerfulness and for giving conspicuous time for prayer and having a place consecrated to this holy exercise. Those familiar with the Bible will recall the many references to places devoted to habitual prayer or to places sought out for the occasion. Daniel had his place of prayer, to which he resorted regularly and which was consecrated to the royal privilege of prayer. Because they were familiar with the places he frequented, the disciples could readily find the Son of God when he would go out to pray long before day. Judas, that fatal night, found him because Jesus often resorted to that place, for prayer and for instructing his disciples. That he had places of habitual resort for prayer seems evident, but that he selected places for the express purpose of prayer that were suited to it is a matter of record. The solitude of the wilderness and the privacy, loneliness, and elevation of the mountains were his closet places, the spots where he wrestled with God and the places from which the great scheme of redemption drew its inspiration, energy, and success.

Peter selected the housetop to pray for its privacy, that he might be alone with God. Christ charges us to enter into our closet, the most private and out-of-the-way place, and to shut the door. We are to be alone with God, dissociated from all earthly companions and all earthly interests, and attend to our business with God. If we are stationary we ought to have one place to which we habitually resort, and which is consecrated to God and to prayer. Using the same place will aid the interests of devotion. The habitual place will kindle the soul into a livelier faith and stronger ardor, will elevate the feelings, and more readily and strongly concentrate the thoughts by the memories of past blessings. The habitual trysting place with God becomes a heavenly place, heavenly air pervades it, and heavenly messengers are there.

William Bramwell, a mighty man of faith and prayer, had a favorite forest into the depths of which he went to meet God and be alone with him. In modern times the student of Methodist history may be shown the little room and the wall still stained by John Fletcher's breath while he was engaged in prayer. Samuel Rutherford could say of the woody, consecrated spot where he prayed, "There wrestled I with the angel and prevailed." Men of God have always felt the necessity of having a place for prayer. Their spiritual woof and warp unravels without it. Without a place to pray they lose more than the body loses by being denied its necessary food. They lose more than the miser loses when robbed of his gold. The most vigorous and valorous soldier cannot always be at the front and with the foe. The hurrying crowd and the pressure of duty and care exhaust the soul, so that the man of faith must withdraw for recovery and replenishment. We are to withdraw for the specific object of prayer. We must make prayer the sole object. It must not be tacked onto other things. We enter our bedroom for sleep, and prayer there becomes an incident to the main object, a decent incident, but still a mere incident. We enter the study to study; prayer may be its companion but only a companion, the interlude of study. This is not making prayer the business and the object, but other things are main and prayer is secondary. Going to a place with prayer as the distinct object and shutting out everything else, high or low, proper or improper, this and this only will make prayer a power in one's life and give to prayer the position that its importance demands. The Christian who is not drawn by a strong inward drawing to a place of prayer, whose desire for communion with God does not make for him a place to pray, has a questionable relationship with God.

How can a man preach who does not get his message fresh from God in the closet? How can he preach without having his faith quickened, his vision cleared, and his heart warmed by his closeting with God? Alas, the message of the one who is untouched by this closet flame will be dry and uninspired. Divine truths will never be conveyed with power. As far as the real interests of religion are concerned, a pulpit without a closet will always be a barren thing. To consecrate no place to prayer is to make an unworthy showing, not only in praying but in holy living, for secret prayer and holy living are so joined that they cannot be separated. A Christian may live a decent religious life without secret prayer, but decency and holiness are two widely different things. A preacher may preach in an official, entertaining, or learned way without prayer, but between this kind of preaching and sowing God's precious seed with holy hands and prayerful, weeping hearts, there is an immeasurable distance.

It takes time to commune with God, so time must be given to prayer, good time, quiet time, plenty of time. Time finds its best uses and true ends when used in prayer. The business is of the weightiest character. The soul must be put in attitude, and this takes time. Sometimes we are far from ready for our audience with God, and time is necessary to arouse our languid spirits. Time to thwart and overcome hindrances to prayer that are outside of ourselves—unseen, mighty, malignant—must be allowed. If prayer were a mere form, a hasty performance, little or no time might suffice, but prayer is the first of duties, the highest exercise, the most absorbing devotion. "Much time in prayer" has been the motto and sign of God's victorious saints. Brainerd said, "I love to be alone in my cottage where I can spend much time in prayer." Luther spent three hours daily in prayer. Rutherford rose at three in the morning to meet God in prayer. John Welch spent seven or eight hours daily in prayer. McCheyne gave many hours daily in prayer. So did Wesley. Prayer is not to be measured by moments, but to give but little time to it is not to pray at all. Jesus Christ, whose example is authoritative as well as illustrative, rose up a great while before day to secure time for prayer. Many times he was in prayer all night. He charges us to be importunate in prayer, and that requires time as well as patience and commitment. Daniel prayed three times daily. He took much time from the business of the state to pray, but the time he spent in prayer kept his politics pure, his state prosperous, and his faith strong. Time and place are necessary conditions of real praying. Prayer without a place will diffuse into thin sentiment. Prayer without time, and much time, will become a dry, hasty, meaningless form.

The Two Beginnings
March 31, 1892

A right beginning to the Christian is half the battle, the surest pledge of final success. A wrong beginning mars the whole work and leads to failure in the end. There is but one right way to begin this heavenly life. It begins in conviction for sin. The character of a penitent must be distinctly marked by every true beginner. To ignore, refuse, or pass this by is to start the wrong way; however pleasant and promising the start may be. One of the evils always threatening the church is that those who have never truly repented of their sins join her ranks. To them the whole spiritual exercise and the struggles of a penitent heart are strange. Modern methods, modern views, and modern conditions have greatly increased the exposure to and the extent of this evil.

In no uninspired book are the right and wrong religious beginnings set forth with more scriptural trueness than in John Bunyan's *The Pilgrim's Progress*. Christian and Pliable are familiar figures. We meet with them almost daily. They are companions with vital contrasts. Christian is serious, sobered by some heart trouble. His movements are slow, the pressure of a heavy burden retards his steps. Pliable is fresh and eager, his step quick, his movements active. He is impatient with the tardiness

75

of Christian, has no sympathy nor understanding of his burden. We have the key to all this in the different ways they started, which Bunyan has portrayed with the utmost fidelity to great spiritual principles. Christian started after this manner:

> I saw a man clothed with rags, standing in a certain place, with his face from his own house, a book in his hand, and a great burden upon his back. I looked, and saw him open the book, and read therein; and as he read, he wept and trembled; and, not being able longer to contain he brake out with a lamentable cry, saying, "What shall I do?"
>
> In this plight, therefore, he went home . . . and brake his mind to his wife and children. . . . "I am in myself undone by reason of a burden that lieth hard upon me; moreover, I am certainly informed that this our city will be burned with fire from heaven; in which fearful overthrow, both myself, with thee, my wife, and you, my sweet babes, shall miserably come to ruin, except (the which yet I see not) some way of escape be found whereby we may be delivered." At this his relations were sore amazed; not for that they believed that what he had said to them was true, but because they thought some frenzy distemper had got into his head; therefore, it drawing toward night, and they hoping that sleep might settle his brains, with all haste they got him to bed. But the night was as troublesome to him as the day; wherefore, instead of sleeping he spent it in sighs and tears. So when the morning was come, they would know how he did. He told them, "Worse and worse. . . ." He began to retire himself to his chamber, to pray for and pity them, and also to condole his own misery; he would also walk solitary in the fields, sometimes reading, and sometimes praying.
>
> Now, I saw, upon a time, when he was walking in the fields, that he was (as he was wont) reading in his book, and greatly distressed in his mind; and as he read, he burst out as he had done before, crying, "What shall I do to be saved?"
>
> His wife and children . . . cry after him to return; but the man puts his fingers in his ears, and ran on, crying, "Life! life! eternal life!"

Christian's beginning is in poverty of spirit; the filth, rags and burden of sin are felt. The Book of God has much to do with his beginning. The law of God, its demands and penalties, awaken and trouble his conscience. The fear of wrath has broken his residence in the City of Destruction, his back is to his old life, his face is suffused with penitential tears and prayers. He has an experience of sin, its heaviness and guilt, which will issue in an experience of pardon, its relief and joy. He has the conscious beginnings of the history of God's dealing with his soul—a history that will make a witness for God and enroll him among the martyr throng.

Pliable entered in after an entirely different way. Neither the burden nor bitterness of sin were felt. The filth and rags of sin were not exposed. No legal fears nor penitential sorrow drove him from the City of Destruction. He had no consciousness of any such city, no apprehension of any such destruction. He entered on the Christian race with all the buoyancy and freshness of young blood and of a nature unbroken by the throes of penitence—not crushed by the struggle at the strait gate, ungalled by the fetters of the narrow way. He was won to the gospel as Mohammed won his followers, by beautiful pictures of future good.

Pliable was an inquirer, not a penitent, he asked questions but did not mourn over his sins. He could go fast because he had no burden of guilt to bear. He never saw his sins at all, neither by the pains of hell nor by the light of the cross. Struck with Christian's description of heaven and its rewards, he said, "The things he looks after are better than ours; my heart inclines to go." He started, and has many questions to ask of Christian, who in answer describes the beauties and inconceivable glories of the heavenly world, its goodly and crowned company, its freedom from the toils and tears of earth. Pliable was delighted by all of this and called to Christian, "Let us mend our pace."

We find the fatal defect in Pliable's religion to be that he never was a penitent. The degradation, shame, and guilt of sin had never riven his soul. The marrow of his inner being had not been pierced. The sword of the Spirit had never gone to his heart. He got religion after an easy-going, fashionable way. He was won to it by promises, by pleasing prospects, by sweet, alluring views, by the beauties of heaven, and not by the fears of hell. He was not propelled by internal conviction but by outward appeals and engaging pleas. He decided, but no sorrow marked the struggle of that decision; none of the repellent forces of the wormwood and the gall were there. All was flippant, bright, easy; a pang of conviction would be out of place, a needless cloud on his bright horizon, an unknown language to his heart. He decided, but the decision cost nothing and carried nothing with it. His race was as short as the spiritual influences were superficial.

Our modern Pliables are too wary and wide awake to fall into the Slough of Despond. In fact, they are such an active and working set that they have filled it up, till no traces are left of this old spiritual landmark. The vitality and sameness of spiritual evils are evident from the fact that the church of today is suffering greatly by this very evil, which Bunyan portrayed so vividly and truly over two hundred years ago. The Pliables who have been brought into our churches by pleasant methods, attractive inducements, and easy conditions, without conviction for sin, without sorrow for its guilt, without an experience of its pardon are the locks upon the wheels of our progress, the parasites that are eating away at our spiritual life.

Feeble Convictions
April 14, 1892

CONVICTION is the first step in repentance, the first breach the soul makes with sin. It is the sense of guilt, of exposure to and deserving of God's wrath, with a sense of absolute inability to relieve ourselves from that guilt or that wrath. The force or feebleness of conviction marks the energy or weakness of life after the spiritual birth. Pungent and powerful conviction for sin will go far to assure permanence and depth in Christian character. A religion that begins in surface convictions may be a thing of sunshine, but it will be a thing of shallows. Feeble convictions will make but little headway against the materializing influences in which earth usurps the place of heaven and rivals its charms.

Conviction for sin is not so profound in its nature or so marked in its expression as in former days. In fact, conviction for sin, which used to occupy so important a place in the history of spiritual struggles, is scarcely recognized now; the name and territory have disappeared from our spiritual maps. Why is this the case? Has guiltiness before God become antiquated? Is sin a thing dependent on changes and conditions? Has a new way been discovered by which the soul gets into communion with God without the shame and guilt of sin? Is sin a myth?

Is God's mercy a fiction? What is mercy without guilt? What is guilt without its consciousness? We allow the weak and unsatisfactory explanation of changed times and conditions to account for vital spiritual changes. Would it not be the part of wisdom to search for a more scripturally reasonable cause? Are not marked changes generally the result of the decay of controlling principles? We should be especially careful to note the causes of change where everything that moves and lives about us is opposed to vigorous religious principles and when all arts are used to supplant or repress profound spirituality. The profundity and intensity of spiritual effects are in keeping with the spiritual agencies used; if these are of the first quality the results will be of the highest quality; if these agencies are of a low grade the results will be depreciated. Genuine spiritual operations may be feeble and insufficient; a drought may be touched but not relieved by a genuine sprinkle. The prophet lamented that God came like a wayfaring man broken in strength and to stay but a night. We do have religious movements and bring in members, but the movement may be without spiritual vigor and the members may be drawn by other causes than "the desire to flee the wrath to come and to be saved from their sins."

A holy church is a storehouse of convicting forces. In deadly hostility to sin itself it impregnates the air with its own spirit. Conscious of the reality and enormity of sin, it affects all who come within its range with the same sense of sin. In painful travail of soul the children begotten of a spiritual church bear the indelible marks of the throes of their birth. A low grade of church spirituality relieves the intense pressure on its converts, and like begets like. The feeble phase of holiness, the obtusity to sin, the secularization of the church, the worldliness, the sensationalism, the absence of the spirit of worship, all these tend to destroy the forces that convict the sinner of sin.

Ardent praying is one of the agencies by which conviction for sin is secured. Revival seasons should be preeminently seasons of supplication. The prevalence of prayer in the church

ought to be like the darkness in Egypt—it could be felt. Strong
convictions belong with strong praying. God struck the center
when he referred to Paul's praying as the proof of the sincerity
and depth of his conviction. We pray in our meetings, but the
praying is sporadic, partial not prevalent. Neither the fact nor
the importance of prayer is evident or emphasized. Is it not
true that the modern revival discounts the travailing spirit,
which gave spiritual vigor to the revivals of other times? Is it
not true that the popular revival has in it more of the spirit of
lightness than of the spirit of prayer? The modern revival is
not, as a rule, born of the spirit of prayer. Lightness more than
prayer shapes the occasion. Wrestling prayer seems out of
place, tears are almost irrelevant to the occasion, and sorrow
for sin depresses it. The Holy Ghost, the convicting agent, is
not sought by fervent prayer, which secures and gauges his
power. Prayer is the native element of the Holy Ghost, the law
of gravity that draws and holds him. Prayer is his triumphal
chariot. A prayerless spirit puts an injunction on his coming
or quenches the power of that coming. The Holy Ghost does
no mighty works and begets no strong convictions where the
spirit of prayer does not rule.

The singing, the words of the hymn, the fitness of the tune,
and the deep spirituality of the heart have much to do with
the depth and intensity of the conviction. Many of the popular
hymns we sing produce no essential spiritual results; they are
not only perfectly innocent as convicting forces but are absolutely harmful. Many of those who are charged with singing
these songs have no spiritual, projecting force. The words, the
tune, and the singers are light and sparkling. They are never
set to the key of repentance—conviction for sin is a discordant
note. Much of the popular revival singing is better suited to a
jolly march than to the pangs of a soul troubled by sin. The
singing of our standard hymns by standard Methodist men and
women who have a standard Methodist experience would inaugurate a new era of spiritual force in Methodism.

Much of feeble conviction is due to the character of the preaching. Modern preaching is pleasant, generally orthodox, frequently thoughtful, fresh, and earnest, but it rarely edifies or makes us ashamed and troubled. Its highest praise is for the people to speak well of the sermon and of the preacher. It is the exception if the sermon makes them mad with themselves, with the preacher, or with their sins and drives them to the secret places to cry out to God against themselves and their sins. Pointed sermons that include encouragements, strong and reasonable appeals, and touching incidents often soften people. Some transient impulses may be felt, some tendencies to good seen, and everybody is pleased. But the chronic, mortal sore is but plastered. The preaching is fatally defective because neither the law nor its penalties are declared. No deep conviction will be secured where the law is not preached. The law is to be preached in a spiritual way. The penalty is to be proclaimed from Sinai rainbowed with the cross. The law may be preached so as to harden, and an orthodox hell may be so proclaimed as to make heterodox hearers. The law and its penalty are to be bathed in the tenderness and blood of Calvary. It is the ordinary method of the Holy Ghost to convict sinners by the law. The relation of the law to preaching was never more wisely nor tersely stated than in Mr. Wesley's journal. To preach the laws in order to convict of sin; then to offer free pardon, through faith in Christ's blood to all convinced sinners. Then to preach the law as the rule for those that believe. "One in an age," says Mr. Wesley, "is awakened to abiding on him by hearing that God was in Christ, reconciling the world unto himself; but it is the ordinary method of the Spirit of God to convict sinners by the law."

The Sermon on the Mount, the Ten Commandments spiritualized, must be poured molten hot into the sinner's conscience. The law when preached as Paul preached it to Felix or as Stephen preached it to his murderers will convict or infuriate men. There is a defective idea prevalent that we must win men instead of convicting them. So we smooth and tone down and discard great sections of revealed truth to make the gospel pleasing to the carnal mind so they will fall in love with it, and it becomes the gospel of lust when this is done. Mr. Wesley was called a legal preacher because he took the thirteenth chapter of First Corinthians and with it laid judgment to the line and righteousness to the plummet, and the hail swept away their refuge of lies. He says of these antinomian gospel winners:

> They vitiate the taste so that they cannot relish sound doctrine, and spoil their appetite so that they cannot turn it into nourishment. They give them cordial upon cordial which makes them all life and spirit for the present. As soon as that flow of spirits goes off they are without life, without power and without any vigor or strength of soul, and it is extremely difficult to recover them, because they cry out, cordials, cordials of which they have had too much already, and have no taste for the food which is convenient for them.

The feeble convictions of these times are not the results of the changed times, or in the change in the essential being and relation of things, but from the enfeebled spiritual agencies that have taken the place of old and honest methods that were so efficient and opulent in healthy spiritual results.

17

Answers to Prayer
August 4, 1892

THE Bible declaration is not only that God hears but that he answers prayer and gives us the thing we ask for, not only in value but in kind. The Bible saints were concerned not only about praying but about the answer to their prayers. The motive and end of the prayer was the answer. They prayed to God because they desired something of him and prayer was valued because it was the channel by which God met their desires. The rule is that God gives us the very thing we pray for. We may, like Paul, pray for the removal of the thorn, which is for our discipline, and God may answer by giving increased grace. We may, like Moses, insist on going into the promised land when God's purposes are settled against it. But these are exceptional. They seem to be but one rare instance in each of the lives of these eminent servants of God, while the reproduction of the instances in which they received the very things they asked for would make up most of the history of their marvelous lives of prayer.

The promise is as direct as the command is terse and emphatic, "Ask, and ye shall receive." "Call unto me, and I will answer." "Whatsoever ye shall ask in prayer, believing, ye shall receive." "Ye shall ask what ye will, and it shall be done unto you." We follow the plain letter and spirit of the Bible when we affirm that God answers prayer by giving us the very things we desire, and that the withholding of that which we desire and the giving of something else is not the rule but the rare and exceptional. When his children cry for bread he gives them bread.

To get unquestioned answers to prayer is not only important to satisfy our desires, but more important still as the evidence of our abiding in Christ. The mere act of praying is no test of our relation to God. The act of praying may be a dead performance. It may be the routine of habit, but to pray and receive clear answers not once or twice but daily, this is the sure test and gracious point of our vital connection with Christ. The efficacy of prayer lies mainly in the answer to it. Elijah prayed earnestly that it might not rain and it did not rain. He prayed again and the heavens gave rain.

The value of prayer does not lie in the number of prayers or the length of prayers, but its value is found in the great truth that we are privileged by our relationship to God to unburden our desires and make our requests known to God who gives relief by granting our petitions. The child asks because the parent is in the habit of granting the child's requests. As the children of God we need something and we need it badly, so we go to God for it. Neither the Bible nor the child of God knows anything of that half infidel declaration that he is to answer his own prayers. God answers prayer. The true Christian does not pray to stir himself up but his prayer is the stirring up of himself to take hold of God. The heart of faith knows nothing of that specious skepticism that stays the steps of prayer and chills its ardor by whispering that prayer does not change God.

Faith teaches the praying ones that God's purposes are always conditioned on hearing and answering prayer. Hearing prayer is God's primary and most inviolate law, and all other plans of God are subordinate to this. God rules the world and administers the plan of salvation in harmony with and by means of our prayers. The prayers of the saints are always incensed before him and the fire from the censer is cast on the earth. Prayer ascends to God by an inflexible law. The answer comes back to earth by the power of God.

Not to be concerned about the answer to prayer is not to pray! What a world of waste there is in praying! What myriad prayers for which no answer is returned, no answer longed for, no answer expected! We have been nurturing a false faith and hiding the shame of our loss and inability to pray with the false comforting pleas that God does not answer directly or objectively but indirectly and subjectively and that by some kind of hocus-pocus of which we are wholly unconscious in process and results we have been made better. Conscious that God has not answered directly, we have solaced ourselves with the delusive unction that he has in some impalpable way and with unknown results given us something better.

We need Methodist saints who get from God all that he has in store for them by the efficacy of their praying. We need saints who can offer prayers that will be so precious and powerful that the whole machinery of salvation will move more vigorously because of the energy of our Methodist praying. We need preachers and people who so abide in Christ that their prayers will help to shape the world for the glory of God. God has an inexhaustible store of good awaiting the demand of our prayers. He has reserve forces, which only our prayers can call into action. Heaven is sick of feeble praying, of languid or icy performances, of saying prayers. God wants men and women who have spiritual needs and great heart-burdened desires, men and women who want much for themselves and for others of that which God has to give, earnest men and women of a true faith and a praying spirit who will come to God with these burdens and desires and will not be silenced till they have conscious, tangible answers to their prayers.

18

Hindrances to Prayer
August 11, 1892

To pray right is to be right and do right and live right. That which hinders prayer hinders piety. When all the obstructions to right praying are removed, the way is open for the most rapid advance in the heavenly life. If we could count, day by day, the prayers that do no good, which neither benefit man nor influence God, we would be amazed at their sum. We must have men and women who can take hold of God and who can draw largely on his inexhaustible reserves of good. The church is being sorely affected by the materialism of the times. Earth is shutting out heaven, time is eclipsing eternity, a bold and specious humanitarianism is destroying worship, the essential idea of God is being depraved. Men and women who know how to pray and who can project God and all his divine institutions with saving efficiency on the world, are our only safety. The church can move with triumph to her final conquests without wealth, in defiance of poverty and scorn, disowned by the world and banned by culture and society, but without men and women who can pray she cannot defeat the feeblest foe nor gain a single trophy for her Lord. Her halls of learning may be closed, her eloquent orators stilled forever, but her prayers will be more potent than learning or eloquence and will assure to her the most glorious conquests. She may lose everything else but the prayer of faith, and this will be more potent than Aaron's rod in calling into being the most powerful agencies and the most marvelous results. In back of a holy, zeal-consumed ministry, prayer must lie. In back of the wonders displayed by the gospel must lie the prevalent prayer, which brings to us with realized power these glorious Pentecosts.

Sin hinders prayer. "If I regard iniquity in my heart, the Lord will not hear me." Heart sins that are not opposed, not warred against, arrest prayer. Prayer cannot spring from the heart that has any bosom sin, that entertains sin of any kind. The thought of foolishness is sin; the glance of lust from the heart through the eye is sin. We must call on the Lord out of a pure heart.

"Holy hands" must be lifted up in prayer. A stain on the hand is as fatal to prayer as sin in the heart. The praying man must be right in his heart and his doing must be right. Keeping God's commandments and doing those things that are pleasing in his sight assures that whatsoever we ask we receive of him. Concealed sins, hidden by partiality or by habit, retained by indulgence, compromise, or culpable ignorance; these, like the worm in the bud or poison in the blood, destroy the bloom and life of prayer.

Pride hinders praying. Pride in some form is native to each of us. No creature has as many reasons to be humble as man; none, perhaps, has so many springs of pride. Pride destroys humility, begets vanity, transfers faith from God to faith in self. There is in pride such a sense of self-fullness that it destroys the basis of prayer. Its constant feeling is, "I am full and have need of nothing." Pride prays, may pray regularly, but its prayers are those of the Pharisee, a parade of self, a catalogue of self-goodness. Pride hides itself under the guise of thankfulness to God, the praising of God with incense from the altar of self. Pride shows itself in the parade of our religious doings, in the display of our religious or other attainments. Prayer must spring from the ground. Pride seeks the highest place and is never found in lowly places where prayer is cradled. The dust must be on the wings of prayer. Pride spurns the dust of humility and covers its wings with the glitter and gold of self. The hollowness of vanity, the egoism of self-thoughts and the egotism of self-talk are all hindrances to prayer because they declare the presence of pride. God, says the apostle, resists and arrays all his armies against pride.

The indulgence in an unforgiving spirit hinders prayer. Revenge, retaliation, the spirit of unkindness, the failure to forbear, the lack of the spirit of mercy full and complete to all who have in any measure or in any way wronged us stops prayer. It cannot move an inch till the sentiment is fully realized or fully clung to, "Forgive me as I forgive." Our failure to hold in the spirit of mercy all the wrongs done to us is the death knell to our praying. We may pray with wrath in our hearts, but this saying of prayers becomes sin. We are liable daily to be wronged in our most sensitive parts. To hold the wrongdoer in the spirit of revenge, or dislike, freezes the heart of prayer. The spirit of forgiveness is the spirit of the gospel, and that spirit must reign in the heart before true prayer can issue from the lips.

The home life, its unity and peace, affects praying. Discord at home hinders prayer. The apostle charges wives and husbands to live in purest love and sweetest unity, that their prayers may not be hindered. A fuss at the fountain hinders the smoothness of the surface and the peaceful, calm flow of the stream. Family discord breaks or unravels all the threads of prayer.

A worldly spirit hinders prayer. The world is more depressing to prayer than all the reeking mists of the torrid zone are to health. It obscures all upward views, deadens all heavenly impulses, and clips the wings of every aspiration. "Ye ask, and receive not, because ye ask amiss, that ye may consume it upon your lusts." Our lusts, the remnant of the carnal mind in us, are the link that binds us to the world. They are the citadel, or the outposts, from which our enemy, the world, has not been driven. We pray, but we do not receive because the world in us would debauch every answer. A pure heart, or one longing to be pure, is the only one that can be trusted with answers to prayer. While our lusts are permitted to remain, they taint our spiritual food. They inspire or tinge all our prayers with worldly desires. To reach God and secure good from him, deadness to the world is absolutely necessary. If we would have God give an open ear to us we must have deaf ears to the world. A heart impregnated or colored in the least with the world can no more rise to God than the eagle can rise to the sun with broken wings. The man whom St. James describes as like a wave of the sea, driven of the wind and tossed, is the man of the worldly spirit whose spiritual energies and decisions are broken by worldly infusions or sediments. He is double-minded, half for God and half for the world, sometimes for heaven and sometimes for earth. "Let not that man think that he shall receive any thing of the Lord."

An unholy life, a bad temper, and any spirit, thought, feeling, and action that do not invite and harmonize with the spirit of God, hinder prayer. A faith disturbed by doubts, or one that faints through weariness or caves in through weakness, hinders prayer. The elements that unfit the spiritual nerve and muscle for the mightiest wrestlings, hinder prayer. We need women and men who live where all hindrances to prayer have been removed—people whose whole spiritual vision is cleared of mist and cloud and night, men and women who have a carte blanche from God and the spiritual nerve steady enough to use it to cover each spiritual need.

19

Conditions of Prayer
August 18, 1892

"PRAYER is appointed to convey the blessings God designs to give." This is a true and concise statement of the purpose of prayer, and so praying correctly is important. Prayer is not just a segment of faith, but it is an intricate part of the whole circle. Prayer is the gathering of all the parts of a vigorous piety and hurling them to heaven. Faith is the foundation principle of religion and the basis of prayer. "He that cometh to God must believe that he is, and that he is a rewarder of them that diligently seek him." Christ announces this condition as fundamental. "All things, whatsoever ye shall ask in prayer, believing, ye shall receive." When a father prayed for his son in an almost hopeless case the reply of Christ was: "If thou canst believe, all things are possible to him that believeth." In the severe struggle and victory gained by the Syrophoenician woman's praying, the marvelous results of that marvelous contest are attributed to the woman's faith. "Jesus answered and said unto her, 'O woman, great is thy faith: be it unto thee even as thou wilt.'" Faith is so strongly the condition of prayer that all the other conditions spring from it and find their efficacy or weakness in the great or little faith exercised. This faith is founded on the ability and willingness of God and rests implicitly on his promises.

A forgiving spirit is of the very essence of prayer.

And when ye stand praying, forgive, if ye have aught against any: that your Father also which is in heaven may forgive you your trespasses.
[Mark 11:25]

This stands at the threshold of all true praying. We are taught that mercy, which had been freely granted, was revoked because the servant upon whom the mercy had been bestowed refused the same to his fellow servant. All enmities must be quenched, all wrongs forgiven, and the fact and heat of these wrongs lost in the great ocean of mercy. The spirit of forgiveness limits the benefits we receive and measures their quantity, for God deals with us as we deal with those who wrong us.

Humility is essential in prayer. Neither pride nor vanity can pray. Humility, though, is much more than the absence of pride and vanity. It is a positive quality, a substantial force that energizes prayer. Prayer has no power to ascend unless it springs from a lowly estimate of who we are and what we deserve. The Pharisee did not truly pray because, though he prayed habitually, there was no humility in his praying. The publican truly prayed because, though banned by public and church sentiment, he prayed in humility. Humility is feeling little because we are little, realizing our unworthiness because we are unworthy, feeling and declaring ourselves sinners because we are sinners. To be clothed with humility is to be clothed with our praying garment. Kneeling becomes us as the attitude of prayer because it shows humility.

Prayers must be hot. It is the fervent prayer that is effectual. Elijah prayed earnestly. Fire makes prayers go, but cold hinders praying. Prayer ascends by flame; heat is its wing. Heat is intensity, not fuss or noise. Fire may not hiss, but it glows and burns. If religion is true it will set us on fire, for God dwells in a flame, and the Holy Ghost descends in fire. The prime condition of praying is to be absorbed in God's will and so greatly in earnest about doing his will that our whole being takes fire. Christ warns us against fainting in prayer. Fire makes us wakeful and persevering and more than conquerors through severe and long conflicts.

Importunity is a condition of prayer. We are to press the matter, not with vain repetitions, but with urgent repetitions. We repeat our petitions, not to count the times, but to gain the prayer. We pray "with all perseverance," hanging on to our prayers because by them we live. We press our pleas because we must have them or die.

Christ gives us two most expressive parables to emphasize the necessity of importunity in praying. Perhaps Abraham lost Sodom by failing to press to the utmost his privilege of praying. Joash, we know, lost because he stayed his smiting. Perseverance counts much with God as well as with man. If Elijah had ceased at his first petition the heavens would have scarcely have survived the next day's meeting with Ahab. If the Syrophoenician woman had allowed her faith to faint because of silence, humiliation, or repulse, her grief-stricken home would never have been brightened by the healing of her daughter. Pray and never faint is the motto Christ gives us for praying. It is the test of our faith, and the severer the trial and the longer the waiting the more glorious the results.

Living well is a condition of praying. A bad life obstructs praying and neutralizes what little praying we do. It is the effectual, fervent prayer of the righteous man that avails much with God. "Whatsoever we ask, we receive of him, because we keep his commandments, and do those things that are pleasing in his sight" (1 John 3:22). Having a constant eye to God's glory and a sincere and earnest effort to please him in all our doing, with hands busy in doing and feet swift to run in the way of his commandments, these give great weight and secure ready audience to our prayers. Our lives often interfere with the force of our prayers and not infrequently act as barriers. Our prayers must come out of a "pure heart," must be presented with "the lifting up of holy hands," and backed by a life struggling and longing to obey God, securing conformity and submission to his will.

> And this is the confidence that we have in him, that, if we ask any thing according to his will, he heareth us: and if we know that he hear us, whatsoever we ask, we know that we have the petitions that we desired of him.
>
> [1 John 5:14–15]

We must, as Jude says, "pray in the Holy Ghost," and as Paul says, "with all prayer and supplication in the Spirit." We must never forget that "the Spirit also helpeth our infirmities: for we know not what we should pray for as we ought: but the Spirit itself maketh intercession for us with groanings which cannot be uttered." Above all, over all, and through all our praying there must be the name of Christ, which includes the power of his blood, the energy of his intercession, and the fullness of the enthroned Christ. "Whatsoever ye shall ask in my name, that will I do."

To abide in Christ aggregates and concentrates all the conditions of praying and crowns prayer with all its limitless wealth. "If ye abide in me, and my words abide in you, ye shall ask what ye will, and it shall be done unto you." To the one who dwells in Christ there is no wrong praying, no wasteful praying. He lives where prayer is born, breathing pure, life-giving air—the place where all the streams and winds are heavenward. He talks to God in the language of heaven, a dialect he knows well. He can pray as the angels pray, and he does the will of God as the angels do it.

Those of us who have too much the spirit of sojourners to Christ are not well enough settled and at home with him to pray well. Too much concerned with our own selfish interests, we are unable to engage the attention of heaven. We are so far away from heaven in our hearts and lives that our voices die away in the dim distance—if they reach heaven at all, they do so as nothing but perishing sounds. To pray well we must live near heaven. To pray well we must be religious in full dress. Piecemeal or patched piety will not serve praying purposes. The forces that impel us to the serenest and brightest heights of faith are the forces that enable us to pray.

The Possibility of Prayer
August 25, 1892

IT is not an easy thing to pray. All the conditions of prayer must support the praying. These conditions are always present with the faithful and holy but cannot exist in nor be met by a frivolous, negligent, laggard spirit. Prayer does not stand alone, is not an isolated performance, but stands closely connected to all the duties of an ardent piety. It is the product of a character that is made up of the elements of a vigorous and commanding faith. Prayer honors God, acknowledges his being, exalts his power, adores his providence, and secures his aid. A sneering half rationalism cries out against devotion, that it does nothing but pray. But to pray well is to do all things well. If it is true that devotion does nothing but pray, then it does nothing at all. To do nothing but pray fails to pray, for the antecedent, coincident, and subsequent conditions of prayer are but the sum of all the energized forces of a practical, working piety.

The possibilities of prayer run parallel with the promises of God. Prayer opens an outlet for the promises, removes the hindrances in the way of their execution, puts them into working order, and secures their gracious ends. More than this, prayer, like faith, obtains promises, enlarges their operation, and adds to the measure of their results. God's promises were to Abraham and to his seed, but many a barren womb and many a minor obstacle stood in the way of the fulfillment of these promises. Prayer removed all the obstacles, made a highway for the promises, and added to the facility and speediness of their realization. By prayer the promise shone bright and perfect in its execution.

The possibilities of prayer are found in allying it with the purposes of God, for God's purposes and man's praying are the combination of all potent and omnipotent forces. More than this, the fact is that prayer changes the purposes of God. It is in the very nature of prayer to plead and give directions. It is a positive force never rebelling against the will of God, never coming in conflict with that will, but seeking to change God's purposes. Christ said, "The cup which my Father hath given me, shall I not drink it?" And yet he had prayed that very night, "If it be possible, let this cup pass from me." Paul sought to change the purposes of God about the thorn in his flesh. God's purposes were fixed to destroy Israel, and the prayer of Moses changed the purposes of God and saved Israel. In the time of the judges, Israel was apostate and greatly oppressed. The people repented and cried to God and he said: "Ye have forsaken me, and served other gods: wherefore I will deliver you no more." But they humbled themselves, put away their strange gods, and God's "soul was grieved for the misery of Israel," and he sent them deliverance by Jephthah. God sent Isaiah to say to Hezekiah, "Set thine house in order; for thou shalt die, and not live." Hezekiah prayed, and God sent Isaiah back to say, "I have heard thy prayer, I have seen thy tears; behold . . . I will add unto thy days fifteen years." "Yet forty days, and Nineveh shall be overthrown," was God's message by Jonah. But Nineveh cried mightily to God, and "God repented of the evil, that he had said that he would do unto them; and he did it not."

The possibilities of prayer are seen from the diverse conditions it reaches and the diverse ends it secures. Elijah prayed over a dead child and he came to life; Elisha did the same thing;

Christ prayed at Lazarus's grave and Lazarus came forth. Peter knelt down and prayed beside dead Dorcas and she opened her eyes and sat up, and Peter presented her alive to the distressed company. Paul prayed for Publius's father and healed him. Jacob's praying changed Esau's murderous hate into the kisses of the tenderest brotherly embrace. God gave Jacob and Esau to Rebecca because Isaac prayed for her. Joseph was the child of Rachel's prayers. Hannah's praying gave Samuel to Israel. John the Baptist was given to Elisabeth, barren and past age as she was, in answer to the prayer of Zechariah. Elisha's praying brought famine or harvest to Israel; as he prayed, so it was. Ezra's praying carried the spirit of God in heartbreaking conviction to the entire city of Jerusalem and brought them in tears of repentance back to God. Isaiah's praying carried the shadow of the sun back ten degrees on the dial of Ahaz.

In answer to Hezekiah's praying an angel slew one hundred and eighty-five thousand of Sennacherib's army in one night. Daniel's praying opened to him the vision of prophecy, helped him to administer the affairs of a mighty kingdom, and sent an angel to shut the lions' mouths. The angel was sent to Cornelius, and through him the gospel was opened to the Gentile world because his prayers and alms had "come up for a memorial before God." "And what shall I more say? for the time would fail me to tell of Gideon, and of Barak, and of Samson, and of Jephthah; of David also, and Samuel, and of the prophets"; of Paul and Peter, and John and the apostles, and the holy company of saints, reformers, and martyrs, who, through praying,

> subdued kingdoms, wrought righteousness, obtained promises, stopped the mouths of lions, quenched the violence of fire, escaped the edge of the sword, out of weakness were made strong, waxed valiant in fight, turned to flight the armies of the aliens.
>
> [Heb. 11:33–34]

Prayer puts God in the matter with commanding force: "Ask me of things to come concerning my sons," says God, "and concerning the work of my hands command ye me." We are charged in God's words "always to pray," "in everything by prayer," "continuing instant in prayer," to "pray everywhere," "praying always." The promise is as illimitable as the command is comprehensive. "All things, whatsoever ye shall ask in prayer, believing, ye shall receive," "whatsoever ye shall ask," "if ye shall ask anything," "Ye shall ask what ye will, and it shall be done unto you." "Whatsoever ye shall ask the Father in my name, he will give it you." If there is anything not involved in "all things whatsoever," or not found in the phrase "ask anything," then these things may be left out of prayer. Language could not cover a wider range nor involve more fully all minutia. These statements are but samples of the comprehensive possibilities of prayer under the promises of God to those who meet the conditions of right praying.

These passages, though, give but a general outline of the immense regions over which prayer extends its sway. Beyond these the effects of prayer reach and secure good from regions that cannot be traversed by language or thought. Paul exhausted language and thought in praying, but conscious of necessities not covered and realms of good not reached, he touched these impenetrable and undiscovered regions when he wrote: "unto him that is able to do exceeding abundantly above all that we ask or think, according to the power that worketh in us." The promise is "call unto me, and I will answer thee, and show thee great and mighty things, which thou knowest not."

James declares that "the effectual fervent prayer of a righteous man availeth much." How much he could not tell, but illustrates it by the power of Old Testament praying to stir up New Testament saints to imitate in the fervor and influence of their praying the holy men of old and duplicate and surpass the power of their praying. Elijah, James says, was a man subject to like passions as we are, and he prayed earnestly that it might not rain: and it rained not on the earth by the space of three years and six months. And he prayed again, and the heaven gave rain, and the earth brought forth her fruit.

[James 5:17–18]

In the Revelation of John, the whole lower order of God's creation and his providential government, the church, and the angelic world are in the attitude of waiting on the efficiency of the prayers of the saintly ones on earth to carry on the various interests of earth and heaven. The angel takes the fire kindled by prayer and casts it earthward, "and there were voices, and thunderings, and lightnings, and an earthquake." Prayer is the force that creates all these alarms, stirs, and throes. "Ask of me," says God to his Son, and to the church of his Son, "and I shall give thee the heathen for thine inheritance and the uttermost parts of the earth for thy possession."

The men who have done mighty things for God have always been mighty in prayer, have well understood the possibilities of prayer, and have made the most of these possibilities. The Son of God, the first of all and the mightiest of all, has shown us the all-powerful and far-reaching possibilities of prayer. Paul was mighty for God because he knew how to use, and how to get others to use, the mighty spiritual forces of prayer. Methodism was born of praying and is a standing proof of its mighty possibilities.

21

Prayerless Praying
October 27, 1892

THERE is much prayerless praying. The attitude and semblance of prayer are in it, but there is no real praying, no projecting of the desires with vigor and in a flame to heaven. The form and show are seen, but the substance and being of prayer are entirely absent. Prayers have been said, the performance gone through, but no real praying has been done. As far as any real benefit is secured, the turning the crank of a praying machine would have done as well. Prayerless prayers are not only a perversion, a waste, a delusion, but they manufacture unbelievers by the score. They get no answers and produce no gracious results. They are vain performances, and others recognize their emptiness and the barren results. Men hear of the prodigious benefits secured by prayer, of the matchless good promised in God's word to prayer, and they mark at once the great gulf between the results promised and results realized. President Finney serves as an illustration of the truth of these statements. He says:

> This inconsistency, the fact that these Christians prayed so much and were not answered, was a sad stumbling block to me. I knew not what to make of it. It was a question in my mind whether I was to under-

stand that these persons were not really Christians, and therefore did not prevail with God; or did I misunderstand the promises and teachings of the Bible on this subject; or was I to conclude that the Bible was not true? Here was something inexplicable to me; and it seemed at one time that it would drive me into skepticism.

When asked if he did not desire the prayers of these people, he said:

No, I am conscious that I am a sinner, but I do not see that it will do any good for you to pray for me; for you are continually asking but you do not receive. You have been praying for a revival of religion ever since I have been in and yet you have it not; you have been praying for the Holy Spirit to descend upon yourselves, and yet complaining of your leanness.

Prayerless praying lacks the essential element of true praying; it is not based on desire and is devoid of earnestness and faith. Desire burdens the chariot of prayer, and faith drives its wheels. Prayerless praying has no burden because there is no sense of need; there is no ardency because there is no vision, strength, or glow of faith. There is no mighty pressure to pray, no holding on to God with the relentless, despairing grasp, "I will not let thee go, except thou bless me." There is no utter self-abandon, lost in the throes of a desperate, pertinacious, and consuming plea, "Yet now, if thou wilt forgive their sin; and if not, blot me, I pray thee, out of thy book," or, "Give me Scotland or I die." Prayerless praying stakes nothing on the issue, for it has nothing to stake. It comes with empty hands, indeed, but they are listless hands as well as empty. They have never learned the lesson of empty hands clinging to the cross; this lesson to them has no form or comeliness.

Prayerless praying has no heart in its praying. The lack of heart knocks the bottom out of praying and makes it empty. Heart, soul, and life must be in our praying; the heavens must feel the force of our crying in order to have sympathy for our

bitter and needy state. A need that oppresses us, and has no
relief but in our crying to God, must be voiced through praying.

Prayerless praying is insincere. It has no honesty because
we express in words what we do not really want in heart. Our
prayers give formal utterance to things for which our hearts
are not only not hungry, but for which they really have no taste.
We heard that eminent and saintly preacher, now in heaven,
Dr. Jefferson Hamilton, speak abruptly and sharply to a congregation that had just risen from prayer with the question and
statement, "What did you pray for? If God should take hold
of you and shake you and demand what you prayed for, you
could not tell him to save your life what the prayer was that
has just died from your lips." So it always is, prayerless praying
has neither memory nor heart. A mere form, a heterogeneous
mass, an insipid compound, a mixture thrown together for its
sound, but with neither heart nor aim, is prayerless praying.
A dry routine, a dreary drudge, a dull and heavy task is this
prayerless praying.

But prayerless praying is much worse than either task or
drudge, it divorces praying from living. It utters its words
against the world but with heart and life runs into the world.
It prays for humility, but nurtures pride; it prays for self-denial,
while indulging the flesh. In gracious results, nothing exceeds
true praying, but better not to pray at all than to pray prayerless
prayers, for they are but sinning and the worst of sinning is to
sin on our knees.

After God Early
June 22, 1893

THE men who have done the most for God in this world have been early on their knees. He who fritters away the early morning, its opportunity and freshness, in pursuits other than seeking God will make poor headway seeking him the rest of the day. If God is not first in our thoughts and efforts in the morning, he will be in the last place the reminder of the day.

Behind this early rising and early praying is ardent desire that presses us into this pursuit after God. Morning listlessness is the index to a listless heart. The heart that is slow to seek God in the morning has lost its relish for God. David's heart was ardent after God. He hungered and thirsted after God, and so he sought God early before daylight. The bed and sleep could not chain his soul in its eagerness after God. Christ longed for communion with God, and so rising a great while before day, he would go out into the mountain to pray. The disciples when fully awake and ashamed of their indulgence would know where to find him. Francis Asbury said: "I propose to rise at four o'clock as often as I can and spend two hours in prayer and meditation." Samuel Rutherford, the fragrance of whose piety is still rich, rose at three in the morning to meet God in prayer. "A wretched system it is and unscriptural," says Robert

109

McCheyne, "not to begin the day seeking God. The morning hours from six to eight are the most uninterrupted, and should be thus employed." Joseph Alleine spent from four to eight in the morning in prayer and holy contemplation. Of the noise created by the earlier rising of those in secular pursuits he would say, "How this noise shames me, doth not my Master deserve more than theirs." So we might go through the list of men who have mightily impressed the world for God, and we would find them early after God. Luther could do nothing if his best three hours had not been given to prayer. Wesley, as we know, was at it at four in the morning.

A desire for God that cannot break the chains of sleep is a weak thing and will do but little good for God after it has indulged itself fully. The desire for God that keeps so far behind the devil and the world at the beginning of the day will never catch up.

It is not simply the getting up that put these men up front and made them captain generals in God's hosts, but it was the ardent desire that stirred and broke all self-indulgent chains. The getting up gave vent, increase, and strength to the desire. If they had lain in bed and indulged themselves, the desire would have been quenched. The desire aroused them and put them on the stretch for God, and this heeding and acting on the call gave their faith its grasp on God and gave to their hearts the sweetest and fullest revelation of God. This strength of faith and fullness of revelation made them saints of eminence, and the halo of their sainthood has come down to us, and we have entered on the enjoyment of their conquests. But we take our fill in enjoyment, and not in our own productions. We build their tombs, write their epitaphs, but are careful not to follow their examples.

We need a generation who seeks God and seeks him early, who gives the freshness and dew of effort to God and secures in return the freshness and fullness of his power that he may be as the dew to them, full of gladness and strength through all the heat and labor of the day. Our laziness after God is our crying sin. The children of this world are far wiser than we. They pursue their desires early and late and in the middle. We are at it neither early nor late, and our midday effort is tame and feeble.

We do not seek God with ardor and diligence. We theorize, speculate, and controvert. We are theological, scholarly, intellectual, esthetical, and petty Christians. We balance theories, debate systems, and discuss issues about the first and second blessing, and miss God in it all. No man gets God who does not follow hard after him, and no soul follows hard after God who is not after him before the day dawns.

If you would seek God, seek him early, and seek him with all the heart. Then he will see to it that the blessings come and that they are rightly numbered and in due order.

23

A Place for Prayer
June 29, 1893

THE pious and devout heart will have a place for prayer. Prayer is our most important business. It ought to have not only time given most sacredly to it, but a place consecrated to it. God is not local, but we are. Places, though, are something to God. He has his favorites that he frequents. Bethel was something to God—more to him than other places—because it was the place where Jacob sought him. Bethel was more to Jacob than other places because he found God there. The revelation of God to him at Bethel made the place sacred, sweet, and awful.

Unless we give prayer a place, as well as time and regularity, it will not be a power in our lives. A familiar place where we have been in the habit of meeting with God refreshes the memory, warms the affections, and quickens our faith. When a place is arranged and set apart for communion with God, we can more easily be quiet there and get to God sooner.

Daniel prayed well because he had prayed "aforetime" in that place. A place set apart makes a specialty and a business of prayer, becoming a part of life's plans and its most serious engagement. The Christian who leaves his place and time of praying at the mercy of a busy schedule will never pray at all.

His prayers may be said after a fashion, but he never really prays. We must, of course, always have the spirit of prayer, every moment sending out our aspirations to God, but unless we root our prayers in regular seasons, a consecrated place, and all the force of habit, we will soon lose the spirit of prayer.

The place ought to be most private—a closet, says Christ, with the door shut. We go there with only one purpose, to be alone with God to pour out our hearts before him. A place for prayer would make our praying more real and more effectual. We ought to go there at regular times, and the times ought to be much more frequent and the stay longer than we are used to. The men who have impressed and moved God, the men in whose lives God has been a mighty force, have had their times and places for prayer. They made prayer a serious business.

Dr. Franklin on Prayer
September 10, 1893

PRAYER is not held in high esteem by many who are professedly religious. They do not object seriously to other folks praying, but it is not a favorite pursuit with them. Rationalism in spirit has entered the church and affected the vigor of its praying. There are many good people who are too religiously active to attend to prayer as a serious duty, a glorious privilege, and a commanding force. We have reasoned away its necessity and force. We have substituted for it a feeble and restless activity.

I hope the following speech made by Dr. Benjamin Franklin will be an encouragement to this great duty. It will show us that the high estimate of prayer is not confined to the superstitious and the ignorant. This speech was made at the Constitutional Convention where men had assembled to draft the constitution of the United States. After the convention had been at work for four or five weeks, and had made very little progress on account of their disagreement on essential points, Dr. Franklin introduced a motion for daily prayers with this speech:

In the beginning of the contest with Britain, when we were sensible of danger, we had daily prayers in this room for the divine protection.

U.S. was born out of prayer

Our prayers, sir, were heard; and they were graciously answered. All of us who were engaged in the struggle must have observed frequent instances of a superintending Providence in our favor. To that kind Providence we owe the happy opportunity of consulting in peace on the means of establishing our future national felicity. And have we know forgotten that powerful Friend? or do we imagine we no longer need his assistance? I have lived, sir, a long time; and the longer I live the more convincing proofs I see of this truth, that God governs in the affairs of men. And, if a sparrow cannot fall to the ground without his notice, is it possible that an empire can rise without his aid? We have been assured, sir, in the sacred writings, that "except the Lord build the house, they labor in vain that build it." I firmly believe this; and I also believe that, without his concurring aid, we shall succeed in this political building no better than the builders of Babel; we shall be divided by our little, partial, local interests, our projects will be confounded, and we ourselves shall become a reproach and a by-word down to future ages. And, what is worse, mankind may hereafter, from this unfortunate instance, despair of establishing government by human wisdom, and leave it to chance, war, and conquest. I therefore beg leave to move that henceforth prayers, imploring the assistance of heaven and its blessings on our deliberations, be held in this assembly every morning before we proceed to business; and that one or more of the clergy of this city be requested to officiate in that service.

Prayer for Temporal Things
September 21, 1893

NOT a few good people are troubled about praying for temporal things. They understand that they are to pray for spiritual good, but they are not certain that prayer covers and controls the realm of temporal good.

Prayer is to affect God, to reach the ear, touch the heart, and move the hand of our Father in heaven. The privilege and benefit of prayer are commensurate with our wants and the authority of God. Whatever is beyond the range of desire for a child of God, whatever lies beyond the control of God, these are beyond the reach of prayer. Everything within the range of a good man's desires, everything in any way affecting his life, everything subject to the control of God, may be the subject of prayer.

Temporal affairs fill up the life of an ordinary Christian. Many of the greatest burdens of the Christian arise from the duties, relations, and business of this life. If prayer may not be concerned with the Christian's temporal affairs, a large portion of his life, marked by the severest struggles, severest temptations, and severest sorrows, is beyond the benefit and help of prayer, and consequently outside the range of God's aid. This cannot be so. There is no part of the Christian's life that lies outside of the range of God's help or of the remedy that prayer affords.

The Old Testament abounds in prayer for temporal things. Abraham prayed that Sodom might be saved from destruction; Abraham's servant prayed and received God's direction in choosing a wife for Isaac; Hannah prayed, and received Samuel; Elijah prayed, and no rain came for three years; Hezekiah was saved from a mortal sickness by prayer; Jacob's praying saved him from Esau's revenge. The Old Testament is the history of prayer for temporal blessings as well as for spiritual blessings.

In the New Testament we have the same principles illustrated and enforced. Prayer covers the whole realm of temporal as well as spiritual good. Our Lord in his universal prayer—the prayer for humility in every clime, in every age, and in every condition—petitions, "Give us this day our daily bread." This petition includes all necessary earthly good. The prayer is perpetual and daily. Each day with its cares and business is to be ushered in and blessed by this prayer. We are to sow with prayer and reap with prayer. We should go to our business with prayer, and through all the day of toil and gain or loss we should pray. We should close the day of work with prayer and end the night of rest with prayer. We should sanctify our days of health with prayer, and sanctify our sickbeds with prayer.

The Syrophoenician woman prayed for the health of her daughter. Peter prayed for Dorcas to be restored to life. Paul prayed for the father of Publius, sick of a fever. He urged the Roman Christians to strive with him in prayer that he might be delivered from bad men. The church was instant in prayer that Peter might be delivered from prison. John prayed that Gaius should prosper and be in health. The divine direction is: "Is any among you afflicted? let him pray. . . . Is any sick among you? let him call for the elders of the church; and let them pray over him."

The apostle says: "Be careful for nothing; but in every thing by prayer and supplication with thanksgiving let your requests be made known unto God." This provides for all kinds of cares.

Business cares, home cares, body cares, and soul cares can all be brought to God in prayer.

The earthly history of Christ illustrates the manner and scope of his operations and the way prayer influenced those operations. He answered the prayer of Bartimaeus and cured his blindness. He yielded to the prayer of Jairus, went to his house, and brought his daughter to life. The nobleman prayed for his son, and Christ cured him. The centurion prayed for his servant, and his prayer was answered. It looked like Christ's main business while on earth was to answer prayer for temporal good. Christ is changeless in his character and the principles of his action—"the same yesterday, and today, and for ever"— and prayer has the same influence with him now as then, entering into the same regions of temporal and spiritual good.

Our temporal matters should be subjects of our continuous prayers. God is the God of providence and prayer. We not only dishonor him but dethrone him when we refuse to pray about our temporal affairs. We can only accept him as universal Lord when we rest in his providence with calm serenity that all things in earth as well as in heaven are subject to his sway.

If we cannot pray about temporal things, then not only is God kept out of the largest and most vexatious portions of our lives, but he is kept out of our spiritual interests as well, for the things that concern this life—its good or bad fortunes—have a direct bearing on the interests of our souls and on the affairs of the life to come. Not to pray for our everyday matters is to neglect at vital points the higher affairs of heaven.

26

A Great Discovery
February 1, 1894

KNOWING ourselves is important but always difficult. To know our sins is even more important and difficult. We do not know ourselves truly till we know our sins. The discovery of our sins will have a more important bearing on our interest and destiny than the discovery of a continent. Sin cannot be discovered by our most searching scrutiny or most exacting analysis. Only the presence of God unveils sin. We find out how unholy we are by finding out something of the holiness of God. We know more and more of sin as we know more and more of God. The sense and sight of sin grow with our sense and sight of God as nearness to God mirrors our deformity and impurity in the fathomless depths of his purity and perfection.

David was gifted and schooled in piety. His genius was sanctified; he was the elect of God, but it took him a long time and a long and sad way to discover the tap root of sin. Poetry, song, experience, prayer flowed richly from his lips. The way God led him was often freshened with silvery streams. He was folded safely in the arms of his omnipotent Shepherd and feasted on his richest pasturage. The satiety and repose beguiled him. The smoothness and beauty of the surface gave no hint of the defor-

mity and treachery beneath. Perhaps he deemed sin but an outward act, a crooked deed, which could easily be put right.

David discovered the true nature of sin by a most shameful
and humiliating process, a process that reached far beyond the
legitimate consequences of his great sin. After he had committed his nefarious crime, many months elapsed before there
seems to have been any consciousness of what he had done
and its enormity. Religious ceremonies and habits seem to have
silenced conscience. Not till God came in convicting power
through a fearless and personal preacher did his act take on
its dark coloring of sin. God shines and David the pious stands
unveiled in his own eyes as a murderer and adulterer. Then
he cries out with astonishment and alarm, "Behold, I was
shapen in iniquity; and in sin did my mother conceive me." It
is not now so much the specific crime that appalls him as the
fearful depths from which it springs, the world of iniquity of
which his sin is but the expression. He goes now in his view
of himself and sin beneath the veneer of grace, training, and
habit. Poetry and sentiment are forgotten as he looks, for the
first time, into the depths of the awful chasm that sin has made
and becomes conscious of sin's inbred and radical evil. The
fountain and the stream corrupt. All the forces, which cradled,
handled, and shaped him, corrupt. He does not offer his human
nature and hereditary taint as excuses for or in mitigation of
his sin, but as an aggravation of his guilt, as a new discovery
of its extent and virulence, and as a plea for a deeper work of
God than that which has yet penetrated his being.

The most difficult lesson for man, regenerate or unregen-
erate, to learn is the exceeding sinfulness of sin, which destroys
all beauty and health and discolors and impregnates with deformity every part of our inmost being. The head becomes sick,
the heart faint; from the sole of the foot to the crown of the
head are nothing but wounds, bruises, and putrefying
sores—all is disgusting and loathsome. If the thoughts, stir-
rings, and fancies of even our regenerate natures were trans-

ferred to canvas, we would not want to see its disgusting, humiliating, and loathsome record.

Many Christians have crude and feeble views of sin because they have no clear visions of the Holy One. They live in the twilight, seeing dimly. They see sin as an outward act and have never seen the corrupt and fathomless fountain from which sin flows. When Isaiah looked on God from a distance, he talked of him and of sin with fluent words. But when God came near, and he saw him enthroned in his holiness, he was smitten under an awful sense of his guilt. His eloquent words fled, and silence, save about his sins, sealed his lips. The terrors of death struck him till God's purging fire burned from lip to heart. When Daniel saw God, his comeliness turned into corruption and his strength into weakness. Job, when heated by the false charges of his false friends, could talk of his righteousness, but when God came on the scene and spoke, the light shone, and Job, humbled and penitent, cried out: "I have heard of thee by the hearing of the ear; but now mine eye seeth thee: wherefore I abhor myself, and repent in dust and ashes."

We ought to be humiliated and alarmed by the superficial views on the direness and extent of sin that prevail among us and emasculate the whole system of recovering grace. Under these views regeneration is scarcely a decent reformation and sanctification a name only. Nearness to God intensifies and expands our views of sin. Sin then is seen as odious and our sense of it becomes painful and keen. The need of sanctifying grace as the complement of regeneration becomes exigent. Striving after holiness becomes an unspeakable groaning. For the average Methodist, God is far away, and sin is becoming a vague and impalpable thing. We must get nearer to God, not to be enraptured as the angels are by the unveiled vision, but to see our fancied beauty curdled into deformity, providing a saving view of our own vileness.

An Old-Fashioned Revival
February 15, 1894

THE greatest need of these times is a revival of religion that will be radical in the principles of salvation, righteousness, and holiness. Times of depression are favorable to this kind of revival. Temporal prosperity, such as has marked the past years, satisfies our desires and intoxicates us with temporal gain. Successes overcharge the masses who are allured and absorbed by the deceitfulness of riches and unwilling to think of the things of eternity. The reign of unrighteousness means that the majority consider holiness an obsolete, an impossible or even fanciful thing. But times of depression have their divine ends that reach further than to legislative mistakes. The wisest human enactments will not bring relief. Legislative enactments can do about as much to relieve us from the disaster of these times as the sentence on Galileo affected the revolutions of the earth. The whole matter finds its solution in a Providence whose reign and results lie beyond the review, and often beyond the ken, of earthly laws and lawgivers.

Men were running wild in their greed for gain. Heaven was getting to be an old-fashioned country, with scarcely here and there a traveler headed there. The depression has checked the wild rush and dashed men's idols (their fortunes) to the earth.

Men are being sobered as well as being crazed. Surrounded by the wrecks of their hopes and fortunes, men are thinking about life as well as about death and are learning the vanity of earthly good. This is a good time for God's preacher to exhort them with God's Word. After the wind, the earthquake, and the fire are hushed, it is the time for the still small voice to penetrate and dissolve the heart and call to repentance. An old-fashioned revival is the medicine for these times. We need to put God in our hearts, in our churches, in our homes, and in our businesses. An old-fashioned revival, which breaks the heart into pieces by the Spirit's convicting stroke, recreates it into the image of God, and fashions the life after the perfect rule of holiness and righteousness, will do this perfectly. The riches of God's grace will make ample amends for financial loss and relieve financial depression in a way and to an extent never dreamed of by the politician.

An eminent minister, writing to a religious paper, expresses it well. He says:

> I am hungering and thirsting for an old-fashioned revival. A good many of us elderly people have that hunger and thirst. We remember "years of the right hand of the Most High." We would be glad to see again, before we die, times of refreshing from the presence of the Lord. Are we wrong in this desire? Has the world outgrown these old-fashioned revivals? Has the church learned better ways of carrying on the Lord's work? This may be so, for we live in the age of wonderful progress. But it will be hard to persuade me that we can get up a better Bible than that of our fathers or that we can improve on the day of Pentecost. We need a great awakening in this country. Iniquity abounds. The love of many has waxed cold. Thousands in our churches who have a name to live give no sign of spiritual life. The children of the church are not converted, and the masses are crowding "the broad road." The church as an institution never had such resources and such opportunities as today. But O for an old-fashioned revival of God's work, with preaching of righteousness, temperance, and judgment to come, till sinners tremble; with singing which breaks men's hearts and melts them in tenderness before God; with conversions that shake men loose from the world, and make

them as bold in righteousness as sinners are in sin! This is what we need. The Lord grant that we may see our hearts' desires.

Such a revival is not a momentary outburst of excitement, not a temporary manipulated stir, not a mere reformation, but a real awakening, a profound and awful conviction for sin by the eternal spirit of God. For such a revival we ought to pray with our whole souls; pray like Jacob, till the day dawns and the blessing comes; pray like Elijah, till the answer by fire comes, till heaven is unlocked and pours out its treasures.

We need a revival that will bring God back to us and us back to God, which will implant in us the verities of eternity and sign and seal our citizenship to heaven. The old-fashioned revival will do this. It will break the heart in twain and fill it with mourning for sin. It will recreate the heart, wipe away the tears, and fill the mouth with laughter. It will make righteousness as conspicuous, steady, lasting, and fragrant as the cedars of Lebanon.

28

Prayer and Power
March 1, 1894

No statement is truer than that made by Dr. Cornelius Cuyler, that "all the men and women of power are men and women of prayer." The converse is also true that those who do not pray are weak in spiritual experience and in spiritual results. They may have other forces, but in true spiritual power they will always be feeble. The busiest Christian workers will be the weakest unless they are busy praying as well as busy doing. The increase of spiritual work will bring an increase of praying, or else the increase will diminish spiritual force. Luther said, "I have so much to do that I cannot get on with less than two hours a day in praying." The secret of the successes of the great preachers who have accomplished marvels has been found in their praying. "When I have heard Mr. Spurgeon pray," says Dr. Cuyler, "I have not been so astonished at some of his discourses." Not to have learned the art of praying is not to have learned the secret of power. Spiritual power is direct from God, and prayer takes direct hold on God and is his power outlet and our power inlet. God surrenders himself to those who really pray.

We use the term "really pray" because there is so much of seeming prayer that is nothing more than seeming. In this seeming prayer there is none of the vigor, none of the fervency, none of the simplicity, none of the perseverance that constitute real praying.

It would be a strange thing to find a Christian with a joyful and strong experience of God, whose life shone out with brightness, who was not given in a striking manner to secret prayer. A preacher given to prayer will be a success. Failure in praying will be failure all along the line.

29

Conviction for Sin
April 19, 1894

A strong sense of sin, of its evil and guilt, is the only true basis of a religious life. This conviction for sin is quite a different thing from a reformation, a resolve to do better, an impression, and a movement. A strong, popular religious tide may originate an impression, a purpose, a desire, an action, which has no foundation in a sense and sorrow for sin and which never results in a genuine repentance. There are many superficial and deceptive influences that lead to some kind of action toward religion. The plan of many a widespread and popular religious movement involves these surface impressions, which have never alarmed the conscience nor broken the heart in twain and cannot stamp the cardinal principles of Christianity on the soul. Bunyan's Pliable was impressed, moved, and he acted, but the impression created no lasting and transforming qualities, no mighty projecting force. The separation in fact and in principle between the young man who came to Christ in the Bible as an eager inquirer and the woman who came as a guilty, heartbroken sinner was as great as his social position, standing, and money were superior to hers; but the gracious results in her favor distinguished and separated them more than anything else.

True conviction for sin means to be arraigned, tried, and found guilty by God's legal process. On this conviction repentance and the plea for mercy are based. The gospel system is based on the fact that man is guilty and needs pardon. Conviction is the pressing into the conscience the fact of this guilt. Bunyan's Pilgrim is a striking picture of a sincere conviction for sin:

> He wept and trembled; and . . . he brake out with a lamentable cry. . . . The night was . . . troublesome to him . . . instead of sleeping, he spent it in sighs and tears.

Solitary, Christian would read the Bible and pray, and being greatly distressed in mind he would burst out crying.

There are so many religious movements that are entirely destitute of conviction for sin by the power of the Holy Ghost that we give the following specimens of the genuine. The first we take from Wesley's journal:

> I preached on Christ Jesus, our wisdom, righteousness, sanctification, and redemption. Men, women, and children wept and groaned and trembled exceedingly; many could not contain themselves in these bounds, but cried with a loud and bitter cry. It was the same at the meeting of the society, and likewise in the morning.

From David Brainerd's diary we extract:

> The power of God seemed to descend upon the assembly "like a rushing mighty wind," and with an astonishing energy bore down all before it. I stood amazed and could compare it to nothing but the irresistible force of a mighty torrent or swelling deluge that with its insupportable weight and pressure bears down and sweeps before it whatever comes in its way. Almost all persons of all ages were bowed down with concern together, and scarcely one was able to withstand the shock of this surprising operation. Old men and women who had been drunken wretches for many years, and some little children, not more than six or seven years of age, appeared in distress for their souls. They were almost universally praying and crying for mercy in every

part of the house and many out-of-doors, and many could neither go nor stand. Their concern was so great, each one for himself, that none seemed to take any notice of those about them, but each prayed freely for himself.

President Finney, in his memoirs, gives us the other instance:

I had not spoken to them in the strain of direct application more than a quarter of an hour, when all at once an awful solemnity seemed to settle down upon them; the congregation began to fall from their seats in every direction, and cry for mercy. If I had had a sword in each hand I could not have cut them off their seats as fast as they fell. Indeed, nearly the whole congregation were either on their knees or prostrate, I should think, in less than two minutes from this first shock that fell upon them. Everyone prayed for himself that was able to speak at all. There were too many wounded souls to dismiss; the meeting continued all night.

We have made these extracts from men who stand in high rank as God's apostles. Laboring in different times under different surroundings and of different creeds, they illustrate the unity and power of God's gospel on the consciences of men. The results of modern preaching compared with these are tame and feeble. Why this? Times have changed is the stereotyped, ready answer. But what have the times to do with God and sin and with the operations of the spirit of God? Is not God the same in relation to sin's dire criminality? Is not the convicting force of God's spirit the same? The models that I have given are scriptural types and normal spiritual results. Our experiences fall below Scripture models and statements.

The difference is in the preachers and the preaching. They preached no dainty sermons, no literary, no philosophical, no heartless sermons. They preached as dying men to dying men. The things of eternity were real and imminent to them. The Word of God was preached with the Holy Ghost sent down from heaven. They were consecrated, holy, self-denying men. God used them mightily because they were in his hands. They had a strong hold on God and strong conviction as to the truth of his Word. They believed in God's law, in God's love, and in his justice. They believed in God's heaven and in God's hell. They believed in God's Word with all their hearts and out of the fullness and force of their convictions they spoke, and the Holy Ghost had a basis, a breadth, and a depth of operation in their preaching. They were men who prayed much, fasted often, and kept themselves in rapport with God. God's creed was not by them abridged; God's spirit not hampered. The Word of God was the substance of their preaching, and the Holy Ghost became answerable for the most abiding and powerful results. The whole counsel of God was declared. God's truth was not toned down to suit public sentiment nor to cover popular sins. It was not delivered in apologetics nor muffled. It was not dealt out with sugar coating nor homeopathic doses. Men were confronted with God's word, were dealt with by God's Spirit, were warned of God's judgment. Their opportunity, their peril, their duty, their sins were set before them; the thrones were set, the books were opened, and they had no alternative but to tremble, to weep, to repent, or to perish.

ارفیہ